LIFE AFTER
CARDIAC ARREST

*Writings from
Sudden Cardiac Arrest UK*

Volume 1

Compiled by
Paul Swindell

With contributions from

Paul Swindell
Sacha Jenkyn
Richard Houghton
Dawn Saunders
Ryk Downes
Imogen Guest
Jamie Poole
Keith Lord
Alex Murphy
David Jeffrey
Chris Solomons
Bob Reville
Mick Schofield
Mark Wendruff
Ingrid Gardner
And Ian

First Edition - February 2018 (e-book only)
Second Edition – November 2018

In case you knew nothing about Cardiac Arrest (NOT heart attack), or thought you knew a lot, then this is the book for you. Written in detail by some of the very few survivors, of whom I am 1 of the 1:10, this book gives a lucid account of what it is like to survive! It will be of benefit to survivors, those who support them and health professionals who may know the clinical details, but not the actuality of life following a Cardiac Arrest. A fascinating read written frankly and without self-pity, this book is enlightening and a must-read as more people survive a Cardiac Arrest

Fay, SCA Survivor

It helps you realise you are not alone! An amazing book!!

Caroline, SCA Survivor

As a survivor of a Cardiac Arrest this was a really interesting read. It is somehow re-assuring to find that other people have had the same problems as you with their recovery, but more than anything it is a book of hope, surviving a Cardiac Arrest gives you a second chance, don't waste it!

Matt, SCA Survivor

An amazingly powerful read. So glad we found this book, my husband had an SCA and it was truly helpful to read everyone else's experience

Nicola, Partner and lifesaver

Great book for someone (myself) who has had an arrest and is confused about how to feel. Sad but also great fun to read there are many other people like myself, thank you all for writing!

Jess, SCA Survivor

After surviving cardiac arrest, remember you are not alone. [It was] great to listen to others experience

David, SCA Survivor

A cardiac arrest is a traumatic event not only for the survivor but all for their family and friends. This book shows the courage and determination of those few survivors and how they learn to cope with such a dramatic and confusing life event. It is also informative on the real differences between a cardiac arrest and a heart attack which is a completely different condition

Keith & Anna, SCA Survivor, Partner and lifesaver

CONTENTS

"Sometimes a little near-death experience helps them put things into perspective."

— ANNE SHROPSHIRE

"And once the storm is over, you won't remember how you made it through, how you managed to survive. You won't even be sure, whether the storm is really over. But one thing is certain. When you come out of the storm, you won't be the same person who walked in. That's what this storm's all about."

— HARUKI MURAKAMI

To Tracy and all the other lifesavers,
You are our heroes and without you none of this would
have been possible x

FOREWORD

W hy do I understand cardiac arrest better than most doctors? Because I understand about neurological uncertainly. After a normal birth and first week of life, my 8 day old son was taken critically ill with encephalitis (viral brain infection) and we were told because of brain injury he would probably not walk or talk. I am glad to say he has done both, if not late and while he has his own cognitive challenges he is an amazing young boy.

Cardiac arrest in my view is simply the biggest insult physically and mentally that a human being and their family can endure. Not only does the heart stop for a variable amount of time, but the cause, the treatment and the resultant quality of life is incredibly variable and the neurological outcome in the short and medium term is uncertain.

It strikes down often completely fit young individuals, with no warning, and your chance of survival and brain injury is completely in the lap of the gods.

Do those around you recognise the signs, do they call for immediate help, do they do CPR and defibrillate promptly, is an AED is touching distance, do you get taken to a specialist cardiac centre? Is a stent or bypass required, which medicines, is an ICD helpful? So many variables.

Cardiac arrest patient care is spread amongst a number of "cardiology specialists" with little collective responsibility or holistic views. Patients are often discharged moving all four limbs, but completely disorientated and abandoned by their care giving teams, whilst looking for many simple answers to complex questions.

This book gives a fascinating insight into the experiences of patients and loved ones who have suffered cardiac arrest and allow us to try to understand the turmoil that patients and family members suffer post arrest, with a medical community which often does not understand the challenges that patients and caregivers face.

I hope this book acts as inspiration for cardiac arrest survivors who are going through hard times. You are not alone. The Sudden Cardiac Arrest UK group is simply the largest and most powerful body in the UK striving to make cardiac arrest survivorship better. We must work collaboratively collecting data, following up patients better, driving governmental change to improve CPR training, AED availability and training, and ensure that all patients who suffer a cardiac arrest get an individualised rehabilitation programme and psycho-social support.

Family members and loved ones must also have access to vital assessment and support as their journey too is laced with challenges.

This book is a fascinating read for all patients and caregivers who have suffered or been affected by cardiac arrest, and for all doctors and healthcare professionals regardless of speciality who might come into contact with patients who have survived cardiac arrest to understand the road along which they are travelling. A road with many diversions, delays, challenges and pot holes.

I hope we can make the life of cardiac arrest survivors and their families better – together.

Dr Thomas Keeble MBBS BSc MRCP MD
Consultant Cardiologist
Essex Cardiothoracic Centre
Senior Research Fellow
Anglia Ruskin School of Medicine

"Your story could be the key to unlock someone else's prison, don't be afraid to share it"

— ANON

INTRODUCTION

This book is a collection of writings collated from the members of Sudden Cardiac Arrest UK, which is a support group for those who have been affected by an unexpected and sudden cardiac arrest. Most of the pieces have been previously available on the group's blog or within the Facebook group.

Sudden Cardiac Arrest (SCA) occurs when there is a problem with the heart's electrical activity, resulting in the heart being unable to perform its vital job of pumping blood around the body. There is usually no warning that an arrest is about to happen and often no history of any heart trouble. The person will lose consciousness instantly and unless immediate CPR and defibrillation is administered, it will cause death within minutes.

An SCA can occur to anyone, at any time and at any age and your level of fitness is no indicator. Although an SCA may be triggered by a heart attack, the causes are different. A heart attack is a "plumbing" problem caused when blood flow to the heart is blocked. Symptoms of an imminent heart attack may be experienced for some time beforehand and importantly the heart keeps pumping and the patient conscious.

The road to recovery can be a long and bumpy one and survivors and families often have many questions. Understanding what's happened can be hard, especially in cases where there is no cause found (idiopathic). In the UK approximately 250 people a day experience an SCA with only around 8% surviving. A person only needs to be down for 3 minutes for them to acquire a brain injury which can result in physical, neurological and psychological deficits.

Ultimately an SCA can be a life changing event and this collection aims to offer some insight into that change and hope for those going through it.

THE BEGINNING

On the 6th April 2014 I was brought out of a medically induced coma to be greeted by my wife and members of my family. I was told that my wife had found me in my office in cardiac arrest two days previously, the morning after my 48th birthday. This was all very confusing to me, but at least I was still alive.

Over the next fortnight in hospital, I was watched like a new born baby and given numerous tests to try and ascertain what had caused my heart to go into ventricular fibrillation - an ineffective quivering of the heart rather than the normal pumping rhythm. Alas, no answers were forthcoming and, so I was recommended to have an implantable cardioverter defibrillator implanted (ICD), which would shock my heart out of this dangerous rhythm should it ever happen again. A day after the implant procedure I was left to go home and try and put my life back together.

After the excellent care I had received in hospital it was a little discomforting to be let home with seemingly no answers or real support in place except from my family. Despite being hardly able to walk to the end of the road and everything taking extraordinary amounts of effort to do I was not offered any rehab of any sort. I've since come to realise this was because I fell between the cracks of the care pathways for cardiac patients. In essence, there was nothing wrong with my heart, it just stopped for some reason and worryingly no one knew what that reason was. I had been told my heart was in very good shape and that the cardiac rehab was for patients who had suffered a heart attack or who'd had surgery. I'd had neither of those, so didn't qualify.

As I had no memory of my event and knew little of what I had been through in hospital I turned to Dr Google, which admittedly, is not always a good idea, but I wanted to know more about what had just turned my life upside down.

Over the next few months I came across various websites and forums and looked at the British Heart Foundation, Arrhythmia Alliance and found that I didn't really seem to fit in or equate with who their target audience was. Yes, my heart stopped temporarily, but the issues I was having to deal with were not really heart related.

I then found a US based health website which has forums for pretty much any condition you can think of. Although not overflowing with information it was populated far more than any others I had come across before. Being US based its main contingent were from there, but there were others from around the world and importantly for me, a number based in the UK.

After several months of reading people's stories of hope and at times desperation there was talk of us getting together. This went on for a little while and then I decided to just put a mark in the sand and see who would come along for a bite to eat and a few drinks in London. I was pleasantly surprised to find that a number of people were potentially willing to travel from all over the country to meet others. We set a date and venue for the end of February 2015 in a London pub called the Mulberry Bush on the South Bank.

On the day in question it was cold and damp and I approached the venue with a degree of apprehension, I'd never organised anything like this before and I didn't really know any of these people. However, I needn't have worried as everyone turned up and there were thirteen of us in the end. The group was a mix of survivors, partners and other family members and everyone seemed to gel really well.

As well as the survivors swapping stories, there were several partners who had also been life savers. It was a great opportunity for them to chat about what they had been through, especially as the actual event itself is probably more traumatic for them.

After the inaugural meetup we continued our chats on the forum, and much positivity came from them. However, it was felt that a more UK focused space was needed and so, at the beginning of May 2015 I set up a Facebook group and then invited all those that had been to the meetup. Facebook has many other cardiac related groups including an SCA group (again this is primarily US focused) and I used these to promote the new group.

Posting in these groups and other relevant places saw the membership of the group grow steadily to over 230 in just over a year and now after 2 ½ years the group has over 750 members.

However, the main focal point is the Facebook group and I would encourage you to join if it is applicable to you. This is a closed i.e. private group where only members of the group can see what has been posted.

We are UK focused and so you should be based here or an expat living abroad, have had a sudden cardiac arrest or be connected in some way to an SCA survivor i.e. partner, parent, close family, life saver.

We share all sorts of stuff and many people who are members have said how beneficial it has been for them - not just from medical issues, but from practical, financial and possibly the most important - psychological.

We do hope that you can join us.

Paul Swindell
Survivor
Founder Sudden Cardiac Arrest UK

NOT THE END

I arranged to meet my saviours seven months after my SCA and I felt giving them a gift was the least I could do for saving my life. I was going through the "baking phase" of my recovery and so I proceeded to make several batches of muffins. While I baked I listened to some music and as I got more into it, the lyrics resonated so much with me that my emotions just let loose. I felt the urge to write, and so I channelled the tears into poetry. As you'll see poetry is not a natural form to me and probably something I'd probably not done since leaving school many years before! Along with the muffins this poem also formed part of my gift to my saviours and I'm not entirely sure what they thought, but it seemed to be well received.

Dedicated to the heroes who were the links in my chain of survival, my wonderful wife Tracy, emergency call handler Tracie, dispatcher Ian, Paramedic Paul, Dr Will, senior Paramedic Ben and all those at the Essex Cardiothoracic Centre.

Exciting and new, the world at our feet
Free to explore, we had it all
Endless, boundless, we could go on

I remember running to the sea
The children playing, shouting, laughing beside me
I had this place to call my own
But just one slip and I was alone

Time was speeding and passing me by
I don't know just what I had done
I don't remember what had made the dark kill the light

Passing swiftly, broken and cold
No time for a goodbye, last embrace, or a kiss
I didn't want to leave like this

So many times incomplete and memories undone

Darkness and stillness, nowhere to run
Not even a silence I could enjoy
If I could speak, I would scream, "Please save me!"
I never meant for it to be this way

My existence sustained by your loving beat
You touch my skin
You keep me warm
And bring me closer to the sun

Saviours summoned from near and afar
Deliverance called to fall from the sky
Hands to lift, to hold me high
And to give me another try

A spark restored!
By your power and calm touch
The rivers flow again beneath my skin
And the savage horses can run again

The torrents grow inside of me
Critical moments are now fading away
But saviours all, in my heart will stay

In the dark, a questioning voice
Bringing me back to who I was
She stood beside me once again
And I knew her face
I felt serenity in all
Heavy waves of gentle love
Soothing whispers from the stars and above

All that we were and all that we knew
Once stolen away with tears and the rain
Restored not by luck
But by a chain of events

You do what is needed
And then, you do it again
Saving a life from the depths of despair

It's not just a body, but a family affair
A husband, a father, a son, a brother continue to be
No hole was dug
No pyre burned for me

My existence was once lost,
But life two has begun
Life two will be my monument
When I'm finally done

Although we have met
Please forgive me, I forget
But because I'm here now
I know you were true
Selfless dedication
Calm and professional
That is you, through and through

Thank you, forever
For your courage
And the things you have done
Thank you, forever
For the bleak hours in the dark
And in the sun
Nothing could be better than just to be able to say
Thank you for being there
On that very fateful day

Paul Swindell
Survivor
November 2014

DEATH COULDN'T SEPARATE US, NEITHER WILL LIFE

O n the 23rd of August this year my husband went into cardiac arrest. We had fallen asleep tired and content after a long day filled with activities, a Parkrun in the morning for my husband while I watched the kids and did the laundry, a nice meal in Colchester with my eldest son, some handiwork and repairs in his house, a weekly food shopping at the supermarket, some gardening for my husband and some ironing for me, and last but not least, the preparations for the next day Skyride, a family cycle event.

I was awoken around 2.30am by a rasp breathing which I first attributed to my spouse having a nightmare. I gently shook his arm with some comforting words, but this time it didn't do the trick. I realised that the breathing was louder than usual – and my instinct took over. I turned on the light. My spouse had his eyes open and was laying on his side, motionless. It was clear that he was not seeing me. I didn't know if he was having a stroke or a heart attack, but I just knew that something was very, very wrong.

I asked him if he could see me, no answer. I asked him if he could hear me, he groaned. I don't remember the next questions I asked while I was jumping out of bed and reaching for the phone, dialling 999 with shaking hands, but I remember the last one, "Do you want me to call an ambulance?". He groaned. That would be the last time he would signal he was with me.

The operator on the phone was seemingly painfully slow. She was asking all the standard questions, name, address, and age. What seemed to be the problem? I was delivering the information quickly, as calmly as I could, knowing that each second was counting, noticing that each of my husband's breath was getting scarcer. I told her that and I was requested to say "Now!" each time he would inhale. I did as I was told. The frustrated operator, thinking that I had misunderstood her instructions, shouted at me for not doing it. I replied sharply that I had warned her- my husband was not breathing. By the way, now. "Again!" she exhorted me. But he was not breathing anymore. Just like that. Silence.

And me. Fear. Blind, sheer panic. Thoughts that I couldn't control, don't leave me, tell me I am having a nightmare, I will wake up in a minute, this can't be real. Then it struck me, I couldn't let him go. I had to get a hold on myself, so I asked: "What should I do?" "You will have to do CPR", replied the operator.

I had to run and wake up my third son. My spouse is 6'4" (196 cm) and weighed almost a hundred kilos. I won't tell you how much I weigh, but it is close to half that and I measure 5'4. I needed help. So, I opened my son's bedroom door, shouted something like "I need your help, now!" and we proceeded to put my man on the floor. Then I started to open the curtains. "Couldn't you do that in the morning?" wondered my son matter-of-factly. "Do it yourself then, and look out for the ambulance" I ordered while I dropped on my knees, searching with the palm of my hand the little depression on the thorax where I had to apply pressure. And I started pumping.

One of the questions I heard the most since then is: "How did you know what to do?" (or it's corollary, "I would never have been able to do that in a million year"). Like you, I saw it in the movies. Maybe unlike you, I had seen the British Heart Foundation with Vinnie Jones, showing what to do. I also had done years ago a course which in Switzerland is compulsory when you want to pass your driving license, called the Good Samaritan course, which teaches you how to save a life. I started singing "Staying alive, staying alive, oh oh oh oh, staying alive..." while the operator, now on loudspeaker, was trying to give me the rhythm with "1, 2, 3, 4..."

All the while I kept thinking. I was two people, maybe three, maybe four, and all throughout. I was the person pumping this unresponsive heart, praying she was doing the right thing. I was the instructor telling my son to open the door to the paramedics he saw coming through the window. I was the wife begging her husband not to do this, not to give up, demanding he'd stay with her, that he'd wake up. I stopped to take his pulse, on his wrist, on his neck, on his groin. Nothing. I started pumping again.

What if he had been without oxygen and I'd "wake" him up, and he'd be alive, but brain-damaged? What if I'd stopped pumping, but somehow he'd breathe again, but would remain brain damaged because I hadn't fought hard enough? What if it was all for nothing? I never stopped pumping.

My husband took a deep breath, opened his eyes. His whole body raised while he was inhaling, as if he had been drowning and was now back to the surface. Then his eyes closed again, and he went back into this deep sleep, this strange absence from consciousness. I kept pumping. "I know you can hear me, don't let me down, wake up for me, wake up for the children, wake up for your girls".

A paramedic entered the room, followed by my son. My eldest daughter had just barged in, sobbing. "Am I doing this right?" I asked. "You're doing this better than I would" said the paramedic. But after a few minutes, I was faltering. He had already open the defibrillator, so he dropped next to me and started measuring vital signs. I was asked to open his bag, extract and unpack the ventilator. I had my back turned when the defibrillator was used. The noise was like in the movies, but the furniture on the floor seemed to jump in the air. By then my daughter was screaming. I told my son to take her in another room and stay with her. And suddenly the bedroom filled up with paramedics, men, women, and I got out of the way, answering questions while getting dressed, fetching medications my spouse had been taking, trying to help, feeling helpless, useless, abjectly redundant.

I don't remember if the ventilator was making any noise, but it was working. The stretcher was built, the furniture was pushed, and material was gathered. I was asked if I were able to come to the hospital. Would I be driving? Should I call someone? I was answering calmly, I was looking in control, I was melting inside, falling into pieces. My head was completely divorced from my heart, one formulating answers, planning ahead, getting my handbag, putting the sheets in the washing machine, checking on my youngest daughter still blissfully asleep and unaware that her world had changed forever, handing instructions for the next hours to my son, even finally getting change for the hospital parking before getting behind the wheel and driving away.

It was by then almost 4am I think. The night was dark, the temperature warm, the streets looked like decors on a stage. Could I drive? I forced myself to stay within the speed limit. My thoughts were erratic. What would I find at the hospital? Where would he be? Still among the livings or would he have crossed to the land of our unbelievable sorrow? If he had gone, what would I tell the kids? What would I do without him? What sense did all this have? I was trying to breathe, I was trying not to cry. One step at a time, you don't know anything yet, keep your head, you'll fall into pieces later, and he needs you.

I will spare you the next hours and the next days of a very long parenthesis in our life. My husband was sedated and placed in the critical care unit of our local hospital. The team was sympathetic, and I spent many, many hours crying and trying to persuade them that this man was worth saving. Romeo and Juliet had nothing on us, I assured them. We were soulmates. This man was the kindest, cleverest, most worthy human being on earth. He was the most helpful, intelligent, useful, charming soul one would ever encounter. I wanted all of them to love him as much as I did. I was warned multiple times that his chances of survival were less than slim, even non-existent. They would try to stabilise him, but they didn't know how long he had remained without oxygen, and they didn't know what had had caused his cardiac arrest. Everybody was friendly, comforting but not reassuring. Every words spoken was wrapped in caution, almost ambiguity, slowly and carefully delivered.

I had to call and contact family and friends. Deliver the meagre news I had. How do you announce to a father and a mother that their son has died in the night, and has been brought back from the dead but you don't know if he will stay put? How do you tell your kids that their father is in no man's land? What do you do with yourself, with your thoughts, with your emotions when they are too scary to consider, too big for your courage, too painful to keep breathing?

It took me a few hours before I came to realise that my husband seemed to be reacting to my voice. I would order him to breathe before the ventilator would kick in and when his heart rate was too low. I would beg him to keep his arms down in order not to break the needles when he would start moving. I would hold his hands when he was shivering under his ice vest. I would kiss his face and his hands when I had no more words to speak.

Then it took me a few more hours to convince the nurses and the doctors that somehow my voice was making it to my husband's mind. But he suddenly woke up, looking straight at me. I asked him: "Do you see me?" and he nodded once. I said: "Do you know who I am?" and he tapped his chest, giving me our signal for "I love you". The nurse grabbed a torch and shoved it in his eyes as he was already laying back. He started calling him by name, lifting his eyelid, and my husband's pupil started fighting the light.

Half a day later he was awake and smiling. Like a child he was repeating over and over the same questions: Where was he? What had happened? Was is a dream, it looked like a dream...Keeping him down, trying to stop him ripping his tubes out (he had oh so many), talking him out of running away was a hard job. But I was so happy, so happy despite the disquietude of the never ending repetitive questions, despite the disconcerting reactions ("What happened?" - "You had a cardiac arrest" - "Cooool...").

Then came the hard part. Because if you think that the worst was behind us, you can think again.

The diagnostic was simple. There was none. My husband, who was very fit and healthy, had had a cardiac arrest for no apparent reason, at the tender age of 38. As we didn't have a cause, this meant that it could happen again anytime. So, a defibrillator had to be installed in his chest. The wait lasted only a bit more than a week, but the back-and-forth visits to the ward seemed to last months. The staff on the new ward was less friendly, schedules were stricter. Our kids were reacting in different manners, some pretending to be fine, some telling me they were not, some being downright aggressive and traumatised. We were trying to talk it over and I was doing my best to keep a semblance of family life and routine. Then the operation took place; an ICD (Implantable cardioverter defibrillator) was fitted in another hospital (Papworth, 70 miles away). And finally, after two weeks of travelling, hospital visits, errands (my spouse hated hospital food) and diverse occupations generated by housework, everyday life took over.

Except that it didn't.

We had had many friends, family and acquaintances helping and visiting at first. I kept our time private as long as my husband was in hospital, diverting helpers and visitors to him while I was doing my best to reorganise my home and get the kids ready for the school new term start – one of my sons was actually moving out and had very poor organisational skills- while juggling with the most unpredictable discussions about life, health issues and whatever it was we were going through. We had tears, mood swings, but also laughs. We watched a lot of movies (hospital visits ended at 7pm) and I knitted a lot of socks. Cuddles at bedtime became a long ritual for the youngest.

As long as my husband had been in hospital nurses and doctors spoke to me and involved me in processes and discussions. I was very happy with that until I came to understand that I was supposed to become my husband's carer. I was expected to stay with him non-stop until his life would resume to a semblance of normality, but also I was now responsible for his wellbeing, for the strict following of doctors' orders, and also in charge for the rest of our household as it was becoming more and more obvious that he couldn't be expected to participate in any household chores or driving in the near future. I didn't know what to think about this, but it didn't take me long to figure out that from now on, I would feel inadequate.

My husband's needs and demands were of course a priority. Helping him to wash, get dressed, were little things meant to pass quickly. I did those tasks with almost pleasure because it was so good to feel his skin under my fingers, to breathe his smell every morning. He was back- that was all that mattered. However, my life became sketchy and erratic. His short-term memory was still unreliable. We would end up with guests I didn't know were coming, events taking place without forewarning. He would forget what doctors and nurses had said and would become upset at the idea of his own limitations. He was angry and frustrated that he was not allowed to go running (while he could barely stand up and walk a mile without going to sleep for the rest of the afternoon). I had to plan every event, weekly shopping, school runs, making sure someone could come and stay with him while I'd be out. I became annoyed with the stewardship and had to ask him to manage his own activities and visitors as I was already overwhelmed with the maintenance of the house and the organisation of my son's move out, the packing of boxes, and the trips to Ikea to refurbish his new place. I stubbornly refused to postpone some of the plans we had had before his cardiac arrest. I repainted the guests room with the help of friends and family, then redecorated entirely the new vacant room in the house. I was advised to postpone all that and wait for calmer times. But I knew better, there wouldn't be calmer times anytime soon.

My husband's first alert was a blood clot in his arm. He complained about it for a while, not listening to my recommendation to call a doctor. We ended up with an ambulance at the door and new paramedics to meet. When they took him away, I cried uncontrollably for an hour. I was so scared that things would kick in, so frightened by the way it happens so quickly, without much, or any, warning. My spouse kept joking all throughout, and it slowly dawned on me that something unexpected was occurring.

So far, my husband has been, since I met him 14 years ago, *my everything*. We have shared our lives with as little absences as we could, and we talk about our inner thoughts, from the innocuous and banal to the crazy, funny and ugly, without hesitation. The word "soulmate" seemed insufficient to describe our relationship: we were one. Most of the time I knew what he thought, and more often than not he could have said the same about me. We shared most of our values, and despite very different tastes in music, films and hobbies, our desire to involve the other into our personal world never faded.

But now came the irony. I felt cheated. My husband's cardiac arrest involved both of us, but it actually divided us. One of us had remained sitting on the fence, and we were not sure who it was. He had no recollection of what had happened. For all it was worth, he had gone to bed one night and woken up three days later. He was feeling punished for something he felt had happened to someone else. And he was growing more and more frustrated and angry to suffer the consequences, feeling weak, exhausted, and vulnerable. To be honest, he had always been active, curious, energetic and enthusiastic. Now he spent most of his time sleeping, and when he was awake, tired. Patience is not his primary virtue.

As for me, and my children, the story was different. We had seen him, to put it bluntly like his GP did, dead in front of us. The violence and the suddenness of the event, the roller coaster of our emotions the following days, the soldiering on and the incertitude that had led our lives since then was just a huge trauma that none of us had yet overcome. Seeing my husband complain about his physical inability to run for the moment looked to me like a very cheap price to pay. His progress in a month had been nothing short of miraculous. Doctors and statistics had been clear: his chances of survival had been less than 1%. Better still, he had regained all his faculties, or not far from it. I felt cheated. We were still reeling from the shock, and he was complaining he couldn't run. It felt like we were in two parallel universes. It was still me, it was still him and the love was still there. But somehow we didn't understand each other. We had been in the same place, at the same time. But how we had lived this had been on the most opposite scale of different.

It is very difficult to see a loved one struggle, and not to be able to help him, not because you don't understand, but because your perspective is very dissimilar. Truth is, I died before, a long time ago, on an operating table. I woke up with a broken rib cage, a doctor who was insulting me because I had died on him (his words) and anomic aphasia (for which I had to do years of speech therapy). But I clearly remember the bemused and puzzled feelings I had confronted to the reaction of people around me. I had no clue about their sentiments, no grasp of the potential hell I had put them in. It all sounded like a dream, a joke or a fantasy. But it took years before I could live normally, and curiously I felt down and sorry for myself for several months afterwards as if I had lost some sense of purpose. Death can happen to you, just like that, without you even realising that it is mowing you down. What is it all about then?

Luckily my husband is a positive man. He not only went back to work within two weeks of having his ICD fitted, but he started helping to organise a charity run for the British Heart Foundation. He began to cook from time to time and is now able to walk up to 4 miles a day. His tests have shown so far that his fitness levels are above what is expected of him, and it is probable he will run again soon, although maybe not to his previous extent.

I live every day one by one. I am not sure I am ready for all the surprises that will come my way, but I intend to go forward. I still don't sleep much at nights, and I don't expect that I will in the near future. All I hope is that either things will improve or that I will get used to it. Being suspended in time is a strange feeling because it seems to take all control out of your life. But time, as they say, is of the essence, because you never know how much of it you have.

Sacha Jenkyn
Survivor, Lifesaver and partner
October 2015

DARE TO DREAM

L ittle did I think as I lay in hospital post SCA that one day I would be sitting here today in this place writing this. At 4am in June 2013 I suffered an SCA whilst sleeping, my partner Dawn woke up by sheer chance to find me face down in the pillow bathed in sweat, but quite dead, ironically the very day we were due to fly to Spain for a tennis holiday.

She turned me over onto my back and phoned an ambulance before commencing CPR. The ambulance arrived 8 minutes later and worked on me for a further 20 minutes before my heart started and I remained unconscious in an induced coma for the following 7 days in the hospital Intensive Care Unit followed by a further two months in hospital.

When the doctors allowed me to regain consciousness I was riddled with Myoclonus (involuntary muscle jerking) so I could not coordinate my legs, arms or fingers. Indeed, the jerking was so bad I could not hold any utensils to feed myself, walk or do anything without an involuntary spasm which was so violent on one occasion it threw me out of bed.

I was moved from Intensive Care to first a cardiac ward and then to a neurological rehab ward. I was still bedridden and placed in a ward with acute stroke victims who could do nothing for themselves, I was so affected by this that to this day I take prophylactic aspirin to reduce the likelihood of a severe stroke.

This did nothing for my psychological wellbeing as I realised that this was exactly how the medical staff saw me, with the same level of dependency and likely outcome and thus my thoughts were that I was destined to live out the rest of my life stuck in a bed, being looked after and observing real life through a distant window.

In fact, I distinctly remember laying in that white sterile bed under those aseptic fluorescent strip lights listening to my fellow patients groaning in pain noting the monotonous boring tick tock activities of the daily hospital processes and crying to myself in abject self -pity thinking this was my life from now on.

Oh how I longed to once again feel the small things in life like the rain on my face, the warming sun and hear the rustle of the wind in the trees, the chatter of excitable small children with huge enthusiasms for what was to come and the birds twittering as they went about their daily business.

I simply wanted more than anything to live a normal life and experience normal things with normal healthy people, but as it was I couldn't walk, speak sensibly or even demonstrate acceptable behaviours because during my SCA I had sustained hypoxic brain injury which had affected all of these things, and now it was me that was not normal nor healthy.

I remember the feeling of being observed, spoken and tended to as if I was a little boy with no will of my own or the capacity to determine what I wanted or didn't want.

I thought that if I couldn't have a normal life with dignity, doing normal things, I didn't want a life at all and I would end it. But before I did that I had to stop listening to people telling me what I could and could not do and find out for myself what would be achievable and then re-evaluate whether life was worth living or not.

I asked a kind but bewildered visitor to find me a Zimmer frame and I got out of bed and tried to walk to the toilet so for once I could pee into a toilet and not a bottle because I wanted the dignity of urinating in a toilet like normal people do. Unfortunately for me my legs gave way and I fell and did some muscle damage, the medical staff picked me up and put me back in bed and chastised me for all the form filling they would have to do. The following day I tried again and fell again and then they then put alarms on my bed and put the cot sides up, stole my Zimmer and offered me drugs to keep me quiet. This was a dangerous cross roads for me, a choice to give up and succumb to a drug hazed half-life or carry on being a nightmare patient until I couldn't.

So I made up my mind and disconnected the bed alarms, refused the drugs and then much later managed to acquire a wheelchair meant for pushing patients in, the ones with the little wheels. But I discovered that if I lifted up the foot plates I could scoot along using my feet. I did bump a few things though and was told off by the ward nurses. But this wily and experienced senior ward sister gave me permission because she thought it would exercise my legs and I would scoot around with a lofty look of contempt for the nurses who had tried to have me banned.

In my wheelchair I eventually got myself outside and used to go and sit under a huge sprawling evergreen tree where I would talk to it like it was my totem or something while I watched the world go by. I loved that tree, and still do in fact... it was my friend, listened to my many complaints and never criticised anything I said or did. During many subsequent hospital visits I always make a point of going to say hello to that tree and giving it a tender pat like an enduring, good, faithful and understanding friend.

I think if you have read this far you might be a little bored by now so I will synthesise the subsequent story as best as I can.

The Myoclonus gradually subsided although never completely disappeared, and both walking out and at home I have collapsed many times causing both bruising and cuts. No one seems to know why I collapse but dehydration, electrolytes and tiredness may have played a part, and I am much more careful about managing this now. Fear of collapsing in public often prevented me from doing things but with Dawns support together with the book Freedom from Fear helped me to largely challenge that negative line of thought.

I have as a point of fact been a keen sailor most of my adult life and enjoy the beauty of the ocean and so to consider that as doddery as I was that one day I could ever sail the oceans again was slightly more than I could have dared.

Or was it?

With Dawn's support or maybe her desire for an easier life I set about planning to go off sailing and knew that in order to be able to do it I had to achieve certain objectives.

Sold a house, folded my business, got fitter and braver, adapted my expectations and then found a catamaran that I liked but the only problem was it was located on the other side of the world from England. Indeed, it couldn't be any further because it was in New Caledonia near Australia which of course involved very long flights with brief stopovers and as I detest airports and flying this could be a problem. If I am honest I probably have some sort of phobia for airports.

Well it proved not to be a problem and I am currently sitting here on my new boat writing this post having sailed 800 miles from New Caledonia to Australia with my long-suffering partner Dawn.

The trip wasn't without issue. 400 miles from land I developed dreadful arrhythmias which made me feel quite unwell for a day. In the end, I got rid of them by jogging on the spot for 250 steps just to bump my heart back into rhythm but this is not a strategy that I would recommend... it was just undertaken in desperation and it worked for me on that occasion. Yes it frightened me at the time, it frightened Dawn as well but I had to know if I could do it and as I sit here writing this I am clearly not yet dead.

I will go and do a download of my ICD and book to see my cardiologist to see if anything shows up and obtain some advice from him which I am hoping will be constructive.

I suppose what I am trying to say is that having an SCA isn't the end of a good life. If you are new and reading this you may feel that this is the case... but it isn't!

We all know life is a risky business and maybe more so now but please don't let the Naysayers convince you that you are better off or safer by not doing something that you think you might like to do... have a go... the worst thing that can happen is that you die trying and what an admirable epitaph that would be. Healthy people also die trying.

I think it's important to each of us to try and achieve something for ourselves each day. Doesn't have to be a big thing just do something, because doing something adds value to your own wellbeing whether that is climbing Mount Everest or growing beans in the garden.

Sometimes if you are feeling suicidal, growing beans in the garden can be a personal Everest so doing it is much more than simply planting beans... The one thing that I hear a lot on this site is people being told that they can't do this or they shouldn't do that. I am not sure that not doing something makes you live longer or it just seems like it?

Many people get old and die regretting the things they didn't do in life and as we all have dreams and aspirations why do we allow other people to tell us not to do the things that we would like to?

You have to have hope and you have to strive to achieve your dreams so when someone who is supposed to know better tells you that you shouldn't or you can't it's because it doesn't matter to them... it's not their dream is it?

Do you have a dream?

Richard Houghton
Survivor
November 2015

Epilogue, June 2016

It's now a full three years since my SCA so tomorrow it's sort of a third birthday or third year celebration and I thought I would do an update to the above.

I did see a couple of cardiologists both of whom were supportive of my plans, although one flatly told me that if I got palpitations again I should take another beta blocker rather than jogging on the spot... but I will probably ignore that and jog on the spot again. Having returned to the UK we sold, donated or dumped pretty well everything we owned. Filled in reams and reams of paper about this and that. Dawn managed to get us a great deal on health insurance cover and armed with 12 month visas we flew back to Australia on the 15th April 2016.

Since then we have done a lot of work on the boat and are now nearing the end of a huge 3 month planned refit.

Early July the two of us plan to set off to sail the 500 miles to the Australian Whitsunday Islands for 3 or 4 months cruising around the Islands of the Great Barrier Reef.

After that... well who knows?

In truth I am still lacking all the coordination that I had pre SCA... still a bit doddery on my feet... still a bit tired all the time... and still very pig headed.

So that's my story of my last three years since my SCA and now we are going to go out for dinner to celebrate because we can.

Thank you Dawn for performing good CPR... for my life, for loving me no matter what and for supporting me in all my endeavours... and thank you the reader for taking the time to read my story.

NEVER FORGET

It's a little over three years since my husband had his SCA. I often say to him that I wish I could share with him the video that runs in my head whenever I think about the events of that night. It was just another day and another night. Unremarkable. We were excited because we were going away to Spain the next day on a tennis holiday. My clothes for traveling were hanging up on the door and our suitcases were packed. I never thought that there might not be a tomorrow. It never occurred to me that what was about to happen, would ever happen, especially in the comfort & safety of our home.

I woke up at around 0300 hours to hear him making incomprehensible sounds. Initially I thought he was having a nightmare, but he didn't respond to the usual prodding. By the time I had got out of bed and turned on the light, his face was flat in the pillow and he had no pulse. I checked 3 times. Nothing. Nada. I remember saying out loud "you've got to be joking"

I called 999 turned him on his back and started CPR with vengeance. He was not going to leave me. I became angry with him because we were meant to be going on holiday. This wasn't part of our plans. I was swearing at him as I was doing CPR, shouting at him too - he wasn't going to leave me.

The paramedics arrived and took control, however as I watched I believed I had a golden thread that went directly to him, and this thread was going to pull him back to life. After each shock I spoke to him "come on, breathe. You can do it" and I tugged on this imaginary thread. It took at least 6 shocks before he responded. But he did. Sinus rhythm and finally down the steep stairs, into the ambulance and off to hospital. I was so relieved. So grateful.

The next six days were spent in ITU and then another five weeks in hospital. A slow but steady recovery for him. For me a focus on feeding him up and doing everything I could to get him better. Fighting for the right care in the right place, never wavering from my belief that he would get better.

I found myself being uber protective, not wanting to leave him, constantly worried that something would happen if I wasn't around. It took me a very long time to feel totally content going out and leaving him. To this day if I am away overnight I am not happy until I have heard his voice in the morning, to know he is alive and well. Ridiculous, but true.

So three years down the line the video in my head still replays that night. It was as if I was having an out of body experience, others playing the roles of him and I. But it was real and a catalyst for so much that is good in our lives today. I cannot thank the paramedics enough. Particularly the lead paramedic who has since told us that he had never experienced a cheerleader at a resuscitation before! He also told us how he was thinking about the words he would use to tell me that my husband was not coming back, when out of the corner of his eye he saw a flicker on the screen. He gave one more shock. The shock that thankfully brought my husband back to life.

It's been a very challenging three years in so many ways, but here we are now having sold everything we own in the UK, having travelled halfway across the world to live on, and sail our new home, a beautiful catamaran.

I cannot turn off the video in my head, I cannot turn off the emotions associated with the events of that night, it's always there to remind me. However, every morning when I wake up I look at my wonderful husband and I am grateful for the life that we have. I try to be mindful and drink in everything I see, everything I experience and everything I do, because I know that there may not be a tomorrow.

Dawn Saunders
Lifesaver and partner
October 2016

IN THE LONG RUN

F riday January 22nd, 2016 started out as any other day. It was day 114 of my "run every day" streak running challenge where I had committed to running a minimum of 10K a day, every day. My body had adapted well and had got used to my daily 50-60-minute run. Only a few weeks earlier I had climbed Ben Nevis on New Year's Eve in the snow, with my wife Bev and followed up with a 10K run when I got back down. On New Year's Day I celebrated with a solo 19 mile run around Loch Leven. The week before I had run my fastest 10K and posted on Facebook that I had never felt fitter.

I had planned to run a half marathon that lunchtime, but got delayed so opted for a 10.5-mile run. All was going well, and the weather was good. I was really enjoying my run. The next thing I knew I woke up in intensive care three days later! I kept asking my family who were around my bed what had happened, all I could think of was that I had been hit by a car. The truth was scarier.

An artery leading into my heart had blocked due to a hereditary condition. This had caused a heart attack and cardiac arrest due to no blood getting into my heart. This had happened just 30 seconds from home. If I had reached home no one was there, and I would not be here today. Thankfully a passer-by saw me fall and started CPR. Others helped and a defibrillator from the nearby post office appeared. It took four people 20 minutes and the defibrillator to bring me back to life. I stopped breathing 3 times at the scene and again in the air ambulance on the way to hospital. I was a very lucky person to survive. There were no warning signs at all, my cholesterol at the time of the heart attack was a mere 3.9. My arteries were in a very bad way though and I required a triple bypass which was performed in February.

My surgeon joked and said he would only operate if I promised to get back to long distance running. That was music to my ears. I had completed several Ultras in the past, but had to retire after 51 miles of the 2015 Hardmoors 60 so I had unfinished business and even in my hospital bed I knew that was my goal. My family were not too sure at this stage but within 24 hours of coming out of Intensive Care after the operation I had managed to climb a flight of stairs. I went home 4 days after the bypass and a week later went for a gentle walk. I steadily built this up until

I started to jog then run again. I had a place in the Leeds Half Marathon and that was my first goal. I managed to complete it with a defibrillator on my back (to raise awareness of their benefits and to money to buy a further three). I ran alongside Bev and my eldest daughter Sherri.

I continued to train most days, but because Bev understandably did not like me running alone anymore I joined a running club, the furthest I managed to run for the next 4 months was a mere 10 miles – once. I thus entered the Hardmoors Princess "One-in-the-Middle" 17.5 miles trail run just to check my stamina a fortnight before the Hardmoors 60 and had a really good run so all was set for my re-entry into the ultra-running scene just 7 months after my triple bypass.

So the day finally arrived, and I was very nervous, but also excited. Could I actually achieve after a bypass what I failed to achieve before? Bev was there as my support 63 miles and 11,500 feet of climb along the Cleveland Way from Guisborough to Filey. The target was to complete the race in under 18 hours. On the way to Runswick Bay I started to suffer. It was far warmer than forecast, my middle left toe felt broken (I wear orthotics due to a foot condition) and my calves were starting to ache. I was only 45 minutes within the cut off so really up against it. I nearly quit at that point only 21 miles in, but thought I would give it one more stage so that I had at least run further than a marathon.

On the way to the next checkpoint I met another runner, Louise, who was to stay with me until the final stage. She encouraged me to start running again and at each following checkpoint we clawed more and more time back. However, as we left Scalby Mills, where I retired last year, my left leg finally gave up and was so painful I could hardly move. I persuaded Louise to carry on without me and called Bev. I was in tears and reluctantly admitting defeat. Bev had other ideas and gave my leg a deep massage. In conjunction with painkillers I was on my way again, but only made the last checkpoint by 5 minutes, leaving me 3 hours 5 minutes to do the last 9 miles through woods and along the coast from Scarborough to Filey in the dark, most of it past midnight and totally alone. I managed to get running again for 5 of those miles before my leg went again with a mile to go.

I managed to get to the finish with just seven minutes to spare on my watch. It was very much a combined effort and something I would not have been able to complete on my own without Louise and Bev. My heart was fine and at no point gave me any cause for concern. My big problem was my calves and shin splints, very unusual for me. After 4 hours sleep I got up for church the next day feeling fine, no blisters and no after effects. A big thank you to everyone who helped me achieve this amazing feat. I'm back!

I now want to give something back to the sport I love so much and have launched the Punk Panther Ultra Marathon Series. Six ultra-marathons all starting from Otley, West Yorkshire in 2017.

Ryk Downes
Survivor
October 2016

END OF THE ROLLERCOASTER

Just over a year has passed since I had my sudden cardiac arrest at 21 years old at my desk and life since has been full of ups and downs. Life after a cardiac arrest is one that can only be described as a roller-coaster which people only understand once they have had one.

I received a phone call from someone who worked for my local ambulance trust a day before my one year anniversary, asking me whether I would be happy to attend a "survivors" afternoon with the crews that attended my cardiac arrest on the day. I was finally at a point where I knew I'd be strong enough to do something like this as my emotions had been very fragile, as expected, in the months beforehand. Being given this rare opportunity has been one of the most amazing things I have done and it's helped me massively with regaining closure on the whole situation.

On the day I met the crew, I arrived at this beautiful manor house in the countryside which really had a calming and warm atmosphere to it which I really needed as I was very nervous! It's a weird feeling going to an event like this because I was meeting people who all knew me, but I had no idea who they actually were and they all had such a massive impact on my life!

There were 8 stories on the day where various people had suffered cardiac arrests locally and were attended by the same local ambulance trust, South East Coast Ambulance. All of the survivors that attended were lovely and all had their own individual survival stories which were all miracles.

The first person that I met was a lovely young lady who was the one that took the call when my boss rang 999. I thought it was amazing that she was invited to such an important event because these people work so hard over the phones and without her knowledge my colleagues wouldn't have known what to do and I possibly wouldn't have had the best chance of survival. Often in the NHS people behind the scenes get forgotten about, so it was lovely to see her get recognition as well.

Gradually, after this the actual crew started to arrive with their families. It was very strange because all of a sudden, I was surrounded by 2 paramedics, a critical care paramedic, an emergency care support worker, a technician and 1 of the 4 HEMS (air ambulance) doctors that attended on the day. In that moment I was speechless because all of these amazing people were smiling at me and you could see that they genuinely cared about me and how I had progressed after the shenanigans last year.

After catching up with all of them it was actually really nice just to get to know them as people and I may be biased but they were all so kind and you could tell that they just loved their job and to them it was something they do every day so they are used to receiving these calls (not commonly for a 21 year old), but they are trained to deal with these things, so they weren't shocked to be sent to one. The day then progressed with us having a rewards ceremony for the crew and watching our "Survivors 2016" video as well as meeting Professor Douglas Chamberlain who revolutionised pre-hospital clinical care back in 1970. He was an amazing man and it was such an honour to meet him!

After an amazing day with these people I realised that that was what I needed to be able to get on with my life and move forward, I wasn't constantly thinking what if, who were they, what they looked like and silly questions like that which my mind was so curious about. I finally feel like after all this time I was able to put everything behind me and look at this opportunity as a bonus and an incredible thing to have been chosen to attend.

I think this is an important thing that cardiac arrest patients and their family should be able to do if they so request to meet the crew because it definitely silenced all questions in my mind as they were more than happy to answer all my questions and my mum's questions about what they did and whether they thought I would survive afterwards (which they didn't, shock! ha-ha).

I was incredibly overwhelmed when I got home and had a cry the majority of that evening and the next day, but that's only to be expected after meeting these people who have given me a second chance at life. I will forever be in awe of these people and how courageous and strong they are in our times of need to make sure we still have a family to go home to at the end of the day.

Imogen Guest
Survivor
October 2016

SURVIVING AN SCA

Like many others on this site I was found and saved by the person who loves me. Who called the ambulance at 4am and who had the sense to perform CPR in the half light of waking from a sound sleep?

Who visited me all day every day no matter what?

Who fed me when I couldn't hold a spoon or wiped my bottom after the absolutely necessary, but deeply embarrassing, use of a bedpan?

Who nurtured me through those many days of my irrational and repeated garbled hypoxic conversations without belittling me by telling me how silly I sounded?

Who constructively advocated for me with the medical staff and made sure I had the best of what was available?

Who tolerated my outbursts, depressions, fears, phobias and forgetfulness with tolerance and kindness?

Who supported my growth post SCA and nurtured my belief in myself which helped me to grow through my irrational period?

I feel lucky to have survived an SCA, but I feel especially lucky to have someone who loves me and whose kindness nurtured me to regain the strength to live a good life again.

To all the Dawns, Davids, Daphnes, Dereks or whatever your name is.

You may never really know how special you are, but **thank you** just for being **You**

Richard Houghton
Survivor
October 2016

THE EIGHT TIMES I DIED

I'm writing this blog because I feel like I need to chronicle my experiences and clear my head. I occasionally can't sleep (like tonight) as it all plays in my head too loudly so I find writing it down has helped.

So, these are the stories of the 8 times I died.

1: Train Station: 20 years old

I don't remember much about the initial cardiac arrest that started it all, only 3rd party stories from my family and friends who had to experience it for me, and some of the bystanders who were nearby when it happened. It was a Tuesday, I think, and I was on my way to my new Internship in the city. It was at an airline in the marketing department and I was very proud and happy that I had got the position. It was 7am, and I was at my local train station. The train station has an overpass in order to get to the platform I needed, so I skipped up the stairs, and rounded the corner onto the walkway. At this point, bystanders nearby said that I dropped down to one knee, and they asked if I was alright. I replied, "I'm fine", but stood up, turned, and walked straight into the wall - before collapsing for good.

I once got a hold of my medical records, and I read the paramedics report. I required over 40 minutes of CPR, 5 attempts using the Defib, and 3 shots of Adrenaline. I was taken to the nearby hospital unconscious, and I was put in a medically induced coma. My Mum is a nurse who works at that hospital, and a colleague saw her name on my phone. I can't imagine how that call must have been. Apparently when she first saw me, they were still performing CPR on the gurney.

I was in a coma for 4 days, and they told my family and friends that when I wake up I will probably suffer from brain damage. Once I woke up, I probably didn't help alleviate these concerns when I asked the same questions over, and over, and over again. Not out of curiosity - just that I was so out of it I was forgetting I had asked within minutes. I failed my first psych exam: failing 1 question - "Who is the Prime Minister of Australia" they asked, I answered "George Bush".

2 black eyes, 1 broken nose, 3 fractured ribs and 2 weeks later - I had been implanted with an ICD and discharged from hospital. I had an undiagnosed Hypertrophic Cardiomyopathy.

2: Friend's Kitchen: 21 years old

It wasn't until a year and a half later that I was dead again. I had taken my computer over to my friend's house for a night of gaming, movies and football - and we stayed up all night doing so. At 6am I thought it was time to go to bed, so I headed downstairs to the sofa. But I had forgot my phone, so turned face and ran back upstairs. When I got back down stairs, I realised that I had also forgotten to take my medication (beta-blockers and ACE inhibitor) - so turned around again, and skipped back upstairs.

On that third time down, I began to feel... "Funny". I thought I was just unfit and feeling tired from the all-night gaming, so wasn't too concerned. I laid down on my bed to try and momentarily catch my breath - but it didn't help. I figured perhaps I should take my medication now, so hopped up off the bed and headed to the kitchen.

I remember reaching for a glass, feeling intensely dizzy and the noise got really, really loud. I held onto the counter to rest, and then silence.

I woke up with my neck at an odd angle, staring at a roof. I couldn't remember where I was, and I felt strangely peaceful. I felt good, like I had just had an 8-hour sleep - which really confused me. My first thought was literally, "Did I go to my friend's last night? Or was I just dreaming I did?" It all felt like a dream, and it's one of the weirdest experiences I've had - not knowing what reality was.

It took a few minutes until I realised that I was in my friend's kitchen, and I had mostly likely had another SCA. My heart was still racing, and I tried to count my pulse with my fingers but came to a number faster than 160 bpm twice.

As this was the "first" time I had had an SCA and been aware/awake for it, I was worried and didn't know what to do. Part of me wanted to crawl to the bench and get my phone to call emergency, but the other part told me to stay where I am, shout for help and not risk it. I chose the latter, and started shouting for my friend to wake up.

3: Outside my Office: 24 years old

A lot had happened in the years since that event. I had moved to a new country (and somehow survived carrying 50 kg of luggage around a new city), and had a shiny new job right in the middle of town.

It was an ordinary Thursday, and I began to walk to the office after catching the train in to the city. It was a nice day, cloudless and sunny, and I felt good - until about halfway to the office when I felt a little palpitation/flutter from my heart.

Having been years since my last event, I had no reason to suspect anything was wrong, so continued my walk to work.

It wasn't until I rounded the last corner, with my office just 20 yards away, that I began to feel out of breath. I felt my heart rate accelerate rapidly, and I had a pretty good idea where this was headed.

I spotted some colleagues across the road from the office having a cigarette, so I thought that if I go and say hello, I could use that as a decoy to try and compose myself and calm myself down. It didn't work.

I made my way across the road, and said hello. I sat down on a ledge, and I must have looked ill, as my colleague asked, "Are you alright?"

I said to him, "No, I think I'm about to have a cardiac arrest."

BANG!

I passed out for a few seconds and woke up leaning on my colleague's shoulder. Unlike the last time, I definitely felt my ICD go off that time. I tasted Iron/metal in my mouth, and my heart rate was still rapid. Scared, I asked my colleagues to call paramedics.

I had a VF episode arrested by my ICD, which started as 10 minutes of Polymorphic VT when I felt that palpitation earlier.

4 and 5: Office Stairwell: 1 week later

Perhaps stupidly, after last week's SCA I went back to work on Monday. I kept remembering my cardiologist's words that if my ICD works, that I should be good to go after 15 minutes. So, felt fine on Monday and had no concerns heading in.

Until Thursday.

I actually still felt really good - I felt no palpitations heading into work, was taking it easy and had no reason for concern. I made it to my office fine, and headed up the stairs to the 3rd floor where my work was. As I rounded the 2nd flight of stairs I got a few steps up, and then...

LOUD NOISES - CAR HORNS - TRAIN NOISES - FLASH.

I woke up and I was at the bottom of the stairwell. I had no doubt what had just happened. Immediately my first thought was perhaps the most depressing and scary thought I've ever had in my life.

"Thank f@!k I was dreaming, it means I'm still alive."

But I knew I still wasn't right. After congratulating myself on still being alive, I felt a palpitation. So far, after an ICD shocks me I feel "fine" relatively quickly - but not this time.

Within 15 seconds, I felt my heart go into VT. I was even getting better at diagnosing myself now.

A colleague rounded the corner and saw me sprawled on the ground and asked if I was okay. I said no.

BANG!

I had a second, separate episode of VF. Speaking to my cardiologist afterwards, after the first VF where I passed out, my ICD administered successful therapy. Speculating, she thought that perhaps because of an Adrenaline rebound effect - my heart immediately went back into a new VT that led to VF and a second, separate ICD shock. I was awake for that one, and I still hadn't gotten use to the sting, or the metallic taste in my mouth.

6: Front Door of the Office: 3 weeks later

So this is where I really started to fear Thursdays. After taking some time this time to relax and recover, I returned to work 3 after my last two SCA.

I was feeling fine again, and had hoped that the worst of it was behind me. My Cardiologist had put me on new, stronger medication, and I was assured this would mean that I wouldn't likely have an SCA again any time soon.

So that's what I thought, until again, Thursday rolled around.

Walking to work as usual, much like the previous times, I was feeling great. I had no reason to suspect anything was amiss or anything was about to happen again. I felt no palpitations, and expressly remember feeling even more energized/upbeat than usual. Life was good.

I turned the same corner as my 3rd SCA, 20 yards from my office - still feeling fine. It wasn't until 5 feet from my office door, when suddenly I felt it. I knew immediately what it was, I'd had 5 times worth of experience now so felt like I was getting good at spotting the early warning signs.

My heart was in VT - 5 feet from my office door.

Scared, my first thought was to get help. There was no one around this time, and I knew I didn't have long. There was a button on the door to speak to our receptionist, but when I looked at the panel, the panel I've used 200 times already - I could not figure out how it worked. I knew this was probably anoxia, so thought my only option was to sit down lest I collapse and do damage.

When I sat down, I remember thinking about my Mum. It stemmed from a comment a nurse said to me the last time - "You know your ICD isn't going to work at some point, right?" - Great nursing. So, this time all I could think about was what I could have said to my Mum if I don't wake up this time.

BANG!

7: My Work Desk: 25 years old

My Cardiologist called that period a storm, and I was now well on the way to having my first SCA-free year.

Life was returning to normal. I asked for counselling to help cope with some of the mental side-effects of my "storm". I was paranoid of Thursdays (can you blame me?), and I was acting out "safety behaviours" because I was too scared. I would stop walking every 100 yards, and I would stop after 3 or 4 stairs, even if I felt fine.

But by now, these were becoming less and less a thing, and I was starting to get "adventurous" again.

It was raining this day, and it was lunch time. Feeling nothing of it, I actually even "jogged" (walked briskly) to the Cafe across the road. I didn't think anything of it, and "jogged" back to my office. I practically skipped up the office stairs, all 4 flights, and actually remember feeling proud of myself.

But this is where it went wrong.

I knew I should have taken a break at that point. I knew I should have given myself time to catch my breath - as proud as I was I knew that it even a healthy person would feel a little puffed after that. But, unfortunately, my HR manager came up the stairs just as I finished, and began talking to me.

While I tried to catch my breath, she walked into the office continuing to talk to me. So, as not to be rude - I followed her in and kept pace. Her pace. I was starting to worry, and spotted an empty chair on our path. How desperately I wanted to sit down.

But I told myself in my head that if I just keep up with her until I make it back to my desk, I will catch my breath when I get there. So kept walking.

And I did it. I made it back to my desk, with my HR Manager still there talking to me. I knew I was in VT - but was hoping that now that I was sat down and relaxed I could wait it out and calm myself back to normal. If only it worked that way.

I can't actually remember what I was talking about to my HR Manager, but I vividly remember what we didn't say.

After a few seconds I began to feel fine, and looked at my HR Manager - she said to me, "Jamie - write your name on the board 3 times" - and handed me a pen.

Except she didn't. And I woke up being cradled and lowered to the ground by my colleague. I died in my office chair. I took a moment to process it while I lay on the floor of my office.

8: Airport Gate: 26 years old

So after all this I felt like I was becoming a pro at dying. After last time, it only took a couple of months to recover and get over some of the mental effects - and I was back in my home country on holiday - as relaxed as I could be. It had been 7 months since my last SCA now, so had once again forgotten to be careful.

In an ultimately serendipitous series of events, my very close Granddad became very ill while I was back home, and we were asked to go to his hometown to be with him. My mum being a nurse, knew it wasn't good when they asked that.

So we booked the next domestic flight up, and had an uneasy flight.

When we landed, thoughts of my own health and heart were far from my mind - and why wouldn't it? - I felt fine. It had been 7 months since anything had happened and the fresh air of my home country was doing me good.

But you'll never believe what day it was.

Of course it was Thursday, and when we disembarked the plane, our domestic airport did not have a walkway attached to the plane. You needed to take your carry on down the stairs, and back up a set of stairs when to get into the Terminal.

Still thinking nothing of this, as I had even done domestic flights previously on my holiday, I made it back up the stairs into the terminal.

While I say I was over the mental side-effects, they have never truly gone - and I still get worried at every staircase I need to climb. So, after making it up these stairs, I knew I should take it easy. So, I began to walk slowly up the gangway, careful not to over exert myself.

Too late. I felt it.

Being the pro of death that I was, I even had a name for this feeling now: "The 8 seconds of dying". I called it this because I knew that once it started I had about 8 seconds until my ICD would charge up and administer the shock therapy.

I made it to the gate - where hundreds of people were waiting for the next flight to board. I knew it was coming, and had only seconds left - so I dropped my bag, and sat down in the middle of the gate.

BANG!

A passenger asked if I was okay, and I said no, I just had a heart attack (I felt that if I called it a heart attack it would provide a bigger impact for the stranger) - and they rushed to the airline staff to get help.

My Mum, who was with me, had disappeared into the crowded terminal, and my phone started ringing.

"Where the f@!k are you?" (She was obviously upset because of the state of her father)

"I died back at the Terminal" I replied

Jamie Poole
Survivor
November 2016

STUBBORN OLD GIT

Two months ago today I had my SCA. 25 minutes of CPR until the air ambulance got to the farm. My wife did the CPR for 15 minutes, first responder took over and they shared the last ten minutes between them.

Eventually was defibrillated and flown away. ICD fitted ten days later. 14 days after rushed in again as a pulmonary embolism put in an appearance. Yesterday I was visited by 3 different nurses at home. They all said I'm lucky to be alive.

I said I feel ok and was able to walk about 50 yards, but complained I felt a bit tired and was told off in very stern tones that I had survived two life threatening events and that I should not expect to be doing much more than walking to the bathroom or kitchen.

They all looked at me stunned when I said I'm a stubborn old git and that is what keeps me smiling and surviving!!

They did the medical checks and shook their heads as everything was "normal"!. The cardiac nurse stayed a bit longer and we talked about how all her "stubborn old gits" were the ones that did best in recovery.

I share this post not to boast about how wonderful I am, but to share with others that it is possible to get over these scary events, by being positive and determined. It has changed my life, we will have to leave the farm and move to a house nearer civilization, but as I shall be 65 soon that would have happened anyway.

So, to all of you who are scared and worried, I am to, but hopefully life will return to "normal" eventually.

Wishing you all the best.

Keith Lord
Survivor
November 2016

LIFE IS TOO SHORT

(To wake up in the morning with regrets)

The Legends & the Commons & Lords

I remember waking up 5 years ago today, excited that I'd be once again playing at Twickenham. I had a hearty breakfast in the hotel and headed down to the Stadium.

The Legends were in the visitors changing room, whilst the opposition were occupying the England changing room. Both teams knew each other well and we'd been in and out of each other's changing rooms to share the banter. It was also special for me as Rory Murphy would be playing at Twickenham for the first time and also playing with his Dad!

Now, I'd not driven to the stadium with the immortal American Pie line ringing in my ears "this will be the day that I die", but I'd arrived positive about the game. I recall introducing the medical team to both sides, Simon Kemp and Barney Kenny, and listening to rugby legend Richard Hill give a pre-match "call to arms". David Rose the experienced Premiership referee was in the middle and I lined up alongside international rugby talent such as Ikram Butt and Henry Paul. Of equal importance were the others on the pitch that day who were all raising money for a very worthy cause.

I don't recall taking to the pitch, nor leaving the pitch by ambulance, nor the week or so after. I've watched the video many times and seen me go down to the ground and then be engulfed by the finest medical care one could ever want. I'd suffered a Sudden Cardiac Arrest, under the posts, after an exceptional run of at least 70 meters (props of the world will understand that this is in fact a multiplier of reality). For upwards of 40 minutes the team worked on my resuscitation till they were happy that I was fit to transport to hospital.

Only between 3 and 8% of those who suffer an SCA survive. Like most, I had no underlying cardiac problems, and post SCA, test, after test, found nothing wrong with my heart, it was just one of those things! As a precaution they gave me an Implanted Cardiac Defibrillator, which sits under the skin on the left side of my chest. It means I can't play anymore, I can't fly a helicopter nor drive an HGV or PSV.

But what it has done is make me realise just how fragile this mortal coil is and that we should enjoy every minute of every day to the maximum. In the early days and as I continue, the support from my wonderful family helped me come to terms with it. A certain amount of post-traumatic stress has resulted in the odd panic attack, which passes in time. I think the SCA was a wake- up call to review how I lived my life and what my priorities were. Since it happened I've been blessed with spending time in India, finding a new group of friends out there, from whom I learnt so much about values, life and living.

I've found that Lancashire is actually a nice place, but Yorkshire is still nicer, and that Brexit and Trump don't really matter that much, and we just need to get on with living. So, to all of you who have sent me 5th Birthday wishes today, thank you, To Helen Murphy, Harriet Murphy, Francesca Murphy, Rory Murphy and Will Murphy and all the Murphy family thanks for your love and support, and to Gary Henderson, Mike Waplington, Bill Thomas, Peter Calveley, Rob Brown, Ian Ayling, Danny Brown, and Keith Kent thank you for your support at the time and your continuing friendship. Finally, to all those friends, too numerous to mention, thank you for being there.

Life is too short to wake up in the morning with regrets. So, love the people who treat you right, forgive the ones who don't and believe everything happens for a reason.

God Bless.

Alex Murphy
Survivor
November 2016

I JUST GET SAD

I stood mesmerised, looking up at the gin -clear, star- studded sky noting the slightly jaunty angle of Orion's Belt. The wash of the passing waves created a puzzling symphony of percussion mixed with cymbals as they slapped and swished against the hulls of our catamaran as she effortlessly glided along under headsail alone in the stiff night time breeze.

In the pinhole pricked velvet sky I picked out the Southern Cross constellation and pleasingly saw the flicker of a shooting star.

I quickly made a wish.

I was therefore surprised and disturbed at the tears rolling down my cheeks.

In my muddled thinking I couldn't understand why in all this incredible beauty I felt a profound sadness wrap around me like a heavy blanket and yet I had no reason to feel sad.

Hang on I thought!

I am here sailing along the Australian coastline in my own boat. I am loved by my wife and have no immediate financial worries.

What have I got to be sad about...And yet I do?

I remembered the feeling of complete vulnerability 3 years ago when I woke up in hospital with someone telling me in unemotional sterile terms that I had, had a cardiac arrest and I was in hospital before walking off without another word.

Heavy drugs from the week I had spent in ITU still coursed through my veins and my first week out of ITU was a blur of nothingness.

My second week was less so, but as I was still drugged to a stupor. I don't remember that much other than the bright white lights and the myoclonus.

Ahh, yes...

The myoclonus...

...that vague and innocuous medical term that describes violent and involuntary muscle spasms that hurt like hell and can hurl you off the bed onto the floor. When they came without warning my body shuddered from head to toe and I felt like Linda Blair in The Exorcist minus the 360-degree head rotating scene.

I had tubes coming out of everywhere, couldn't feed myself .In fact, I couldn't hold a spoon or anything else because I would spasm and throw it somewhere.

Hang on!

If I cannot feed myself, look after myself, have to urinate through a catheter and be fed through a tube!

I am done...

Finished...

My life is over and I will never again feel a cold New York winter wind slash my face or see the warm summer rain bring a special fresh beauty to a wild meadow, the buzz of a bee or listen to the dawn chorus in an early morning spring.

I am done...

Finished...

Forever dependent on people who care for a living because I am destined to spend the rest of my life in a bed or a chair observing life through a distant window that I am unable to open.

I am done...

Tick-tock... tick-tock... tick-tock... tick-tock... the monotony of the dreary days passed as if time had slowed to a stop.

The whiteness of the ward, lack of plants, flowers, paintings and anaemic looking tea which came twice per day as did the medications trolley merely added to the institutional perspective on routine and asepsis.

It was sterile in every sense of the word...

...sterile for the germs and sterile for the brain.

My wife brought me in a portable DVD player and paid for T.V. on the swinging over bedside unit and I watched many films wearing headphones to fill the void in between her daily visits. These were really helpful to me as during the cardiac arrest I had suffered some hypoxic brain injury and my socialisation was disturbed, meaning I lost the skill and social rules guiding ordinary conversations.

I interrupted people, did not listen to what they were saying, and topic hopped more often than Freddy the frog. Tell me about your dying Aunty and I would be just as likely to tell you my favourite ice cream flavour.

Tell me how affected you were when you were made redundant after 30 years loyal service and I would start searching for the TV remote. I simply couldn't link and respond like most people are expected to.

Empathy, compassion and understanding had disappeared to be replaced by...
...well... nothing!

So for me to simply watch the way people interacted on TV was an incredible learning tool from which I benefited greatly (I hope).

I unwittingly started to associate between behaviours and conversations, meaning and implications. So the day when the doctor told me I had to have an ICD fitted I knew I should listen and I knew I should ask him some useful questions instead of telling him I once had a dog called Pru.

One day a nurse appeared by my bed to remove my catheter but I had decided I wanted to do that myself and remember feeling surprised by how pain free it was as I gingerly removed it.

In a weird way I felt good about that experience because for me it was a measure of progress as I now could pee into a bottle and I got a little beyond myself.

I decided I could now climb Everest and although at this point I had never been out of bed I managed to somehow get hold of a Zimmer frame and walk (or shuffle) to the toilet like ordinary people did because I now wanted the dignity of urinating into a toilet and not a cardboard bottle.

Unfortunately as I stood there my legs gave way mid-stream and I fell twisting one leg underneath me in a kind of unpractised and painful advanced yoga move, and I tore something in my knee. Much screaming later a male nurse called Josh arrived and somehow sorted me out the poor blighter.

When Josh had got me back into bed I was told off in no uncertain terms about the consequences of my folly and unsurprisingly moved shortly afterwards to a rehabilitation ward.

On the face of it this was indeed progress especially as I was in part bribed by the suggestion that they had a therapeutic swimming pool to which I would have access (although this never happened).

What they didn't tell me was the ward was occupied by stroke survivors who either couldn't move, or couldn't speak, and after the initial shock the realisation descended upon me that this is how they see me... and if this is how they see me then perhaps... this is how I am... and my prospects for recovery were as dim as a spent candle.

I frequently experienced suicidal thoughts.

On getting to the ward they had obviously been briefed about me so they alarmed my bed so that if I moved they would be notified and as a side my Zimmer was confiscated.

The bed sides were put up and then they left me.

I festered for a while listening to the whimpering of my fellow patients until I threw a tantrum, and slid out the alarm cushions and lobbed them causing a rushed response to my bedside to which I declared that I would NOT be sleeping on alarm cushions and I wanted my Zimmer back.

Well the Zimmer didn't return, but a small wheeled wheelchair did and I set about exploring the hospital by lifting the foot plates and scooting with my feet.

My myoclonus had improved, but not disappeared and I was still very prone to falling, however the wheelchair allowed me to push it empty when I could and sit in it when I needed.

With my wife's help I also got to go outside which is where I used to go and sit under the most awesome weeping willow I had ever seen.

I loved that tree (and still do) it became my best friend through some very dark days.

After two months during which I had improved I discharged myself and went home with my wife and a wheelchair!

I fell and injured myself many times trying to do things that were beyond me.

One day I decided to paint the garage woodwork but ended up with two litres of gloss paint over me and the floor and a huge gash in my forehead :(

So why during one starry nights sail in Australia when I am all alone surrounded in abject beauty and wonderment, doing the thing I love...

...do I well up and feel incredibly sad?

Well because I cannot stop myself remembering what happened... and how but for a flicker of fate, I wouldn't be here to experience this wonderful life filled with wonderful people and sometimes...

...just sometimes...

...I feel sad.

Maybe seize the day, live for the moment, every breath you take, every experience...

...all have a place and it is indeed a good if not a great place to be.

But also maybe reflection and sadness have their place for us SCA survivors. Maybe it's all part of the bereavement process where we lament a past life where you didn't fall, didn't have shocks or could drive, walk or work without any worries. A life where you didn't have to be socially cautious or embarrassed because your stamina isn't what it used to be.

A life of good health and well- being.

During my SCA I lost some of these things.

But I also gained some things that I wouldn't have done but for the SCA.

I have learned deeper humility and gained greater compassion for those less fortunate than me.

I appreciate more of my life than I ever did and I think I have much more understanding of what love is.

But occasionally...

...just occasionally,

and I don't know why...

...I just get sad...

...having once died I can now live with that I think?

Richard Houghton
Survivor
December 2016

ALTERED MINDS

I t's odd being an SCA survivor because you do seem to think differently to how you used to. I was stood on a platform yesterday 6ft high using an angle grinder on our boat hull.

Firstly I noted that the on switch locked on which meant if I dropped it then it might not turn off. That's fine I suppose unless it fell on me which wouldn't be fun.

Then I wondered if the magnets in the electric motor affected my ICD.

Well I didn't fall and my ICD didn't bleep so I assume that's okay, but it got me to thinking about quite how much an SCA affects our daily thinking.

I realised how it affects my EVERY thought in that in anything I do or in some cases do not do the SCA calculations in my mind constantly takes place like a computer cooling fan humming away in the background.

I go for a walk and wonder if it will be too long or hilly and I will collapse, but on the other hand I know the walk will be good for me, but on the other hand it might be too far, but... and so it goes on...

Do something strenuous and wonder if my heart will be okay?

Go into someone's kitchen and look at the hob to see if it's an induction hob, caution, caution, caution...

While using an electric tool with a motor.

Climbing or descending a ladder etc etc...

The list goes on forever really and while these thoughts of self-preservation churn around in my mind I cannot help but wonder if it's the same for everyone with some ailment.

The blind leaving their home.
The epileptics going through a bad patch.
The diabetics at a social function.

Do all people generally unwittingly exhibit a cautious attitude to everyday life (beyond the obvious) and my/our extra considerations are just a bolt on to that?

I don't know, but it's an interesting thought that I have never really crystallised before that people with an ailment live with the low level hum of the stress of having to pre-mortem pretty well everything they do precisely because of their ailment

Behaving a little like a soldier moving through hostile territory always on his/her guard that an attack could come at any moment from anywhere and they need to be in a constant state of readiness.

He/she keeps their head together but does it eventually take its toll I wonder?

Richard Houghton
Survivor
February 2017

SEVEN MINUTES

The following is an extract from "The Long Path to Me", a book that the author, David Jeffrey has published since the original publication of this book. The book details his journey through his therapy for the deep scar that cancer has gouged on him and his family. The piece below is subsequent to the books main story, hence the opening "epilogue".

Epilogue

Seven minutes of my life are missing.
All is black.
All is silent.

There is no consciousness, no awareness, no realisation of unconsciousness.
It is silent, amorphous, a world without verbs or adjectives.
None are possible.
They don't exist.
Neither do I.

"Hello! Can you hear me David?" I do not respond. "Can you hear me David? Do you know where you are?" There is a bemused look on my face. I still don't respond. "Lie down David and try to relax, we're here to help you"

Reality seems strange, it's as if I am now dreaming, but dreaming in black and white, a fuzzy black and white. I can hear people speaking but the words make no sense to me. I am sitting on the tiles by the side of a swimming pool clothed in just my swimming trunks, my goggles are on my upper arm. I am surrounded by people. Some are in their swimwear, some clothed.

Reality disappears.
It returns.

The ceiling and lights fade in from nowhere, colour partially restored. I look across the swimming pool. What am I doing sitting here when I should be swimming? Pain is searing through my rib-cage, its intensity changing with each breath. Confusion still overcomes me.

Sleep.
I need to sleep.
I need to finish this dream.
I want to wake to the proper reality.

Someone is kneeling, looking at me, talking to me. He is wearing green. His mouth is moving, words are escaping and traveling towards my ears. They fail to gain entry. I have lost the ability to comprehend.

Unconsciousness engulfs me, the dream has disappeared, and I see the blackness of nothing. I have returned to my world devoid of verbs and adjectives.

Time has no meaning in my world, for tracking the intervals of a clock ticking would require consciousness and perception and I have none. Instead I exist, yet do not exist, in nothing.

I am awake, I can see reality in faded colour, a fuzzy TV picture.
I am lying down.
I am outside.
I am talking, conversing.
I am asking why the road is so quiet.
This is London, in place of the rumble of traffic there is only silence.
This is not normal.
The police have closed the road.
Reality is proving to be unreal for me. I want sleep again.
A solitary vehicle moves, twists, turns, and then lurches forward.
A destination beckons.
A blue light flashes.
A siren sounds its signature.
I fall into a deep sleep.

My slumber, if it could be described as such, recedes and a reality returned to me. I am warm and comfortable, lying in a bed. I open my eyes and the ceiling comes into view. A cannula protrudes from my right hand, another in my forearm, the latter being attached to a thin plastic tube, a bag of colourless liquid is feeding its content into my arm. My chest is littered with small electrodes, each attached to a coloured cable, the monitor above my head absorbing their signals. Below my right collar bone sits a large white rectangular pad, another identical pad covered my lower left ribs, their significance not apparent to me.

As if from nowhere a man appears, he is dressed in light green cotton, a mask is around his neck, and then a second similarly attired person joins him.

"Hello. How are you feeling?"
Yet again I am confused.

Someone replies, it sounds like my voice, the words are coming from me, but I am not conscious of having decided to speak. I want the voice to stop so that I can reply.

"Err. I feel....err...."
The voice sounds in synchronicity with my desire then stops.

I start to speak. The same voice appears, and I realise that it is mine, that I am in control of it, that I am providing the words

"Where am I? What am I doing here?"

The first man dressed in green speaks, his terminology medical.
"Well, you are a very lucky man. You had cardiac arrest after your swim. We checked you over, one of the arteries on your heart was narrowed, not occluded, so we put a stent in it as a precaution. Unlikely to cause and arrest, but then you presented as such. How are you feeling?"

My humour returns "Well, I have felt better. My ribs hurt. It feels like I have been hit with a sledge hammer"

"That would have been the CPR, often ribs are cracked during chest compressions. A small price to pay, wouldn't you agree".

My reality has just expanded. Cardiac-arrest and now CPR.

"It's hard to tell if you had a heart-attack or not but you certainly suffered cardiac arrest and it looks like they did two rounds of CPR on you and then one shock from a defibrillator. You were extremely lucky as it looks like the gym staff were well trained and had a defibrillator and knew how to use it"

My comprehension of the events of the previous hours are clouded by morphine and Midazolam. His words seem unreal to me, they drift around my mind until finding refuge from the medication and I can understand their meaning. As the morphine induced warmth returns to my mind I smile as I reflect on the medic's words.

I question myself, the internal dialogue within demanding answers. I nearly died, my heart stopped beating, someone resuscitated me, and someone revived me.

Where did this all happen?
Who saved me?
How did I get here?

Medication applies its benefit once again and I slip into a warm and delicious sleep.

The day had started just like any other ordinary day via the shrill tones of my bedside alarm clock at 05:35. I slipped into my standard routine of exiting my bed and occupying the shower for some all-too-brief minutes. Showered and shaved I descended the stairs to my home office, where in a built-in cupboard resided my shirts and suits. I selected a white shirt, double-cuffed, gleaming resplendently on its hanger and I slipped into it. Alongside the shirts sat my suits, depending on which one was worn the previous day would determine my choice for that day, I selected my favourite navy Ede and Ravenscroft two-piece, and lowered myself into the trousers. With my tie affixed and shoes placed on my feet I pulled on my jacket and exited the house. I was expecting an ordinary day at work (although I was still excited from the previous evening event's where I had played on stage in a band for the first time ever, my skill on guitar and vocals exceeding everyone's expectations).

The morning was fresh, long shadows of the low sun greeted my train on its journey to London. The spires of city came into site as my carriage slid through the southern suburbs, my destination of Waterloo station approached. After a brief subterranean transit, I was deposited in the heart of the City of London, within minutes I was sitting at my desk on the 7th floor of a stone office building. Bag and jacket deposited I descended in the building's lift to the basement.

Breakfast had beckoned since the first tone of my alarm clock and I wanted to diminish my hunger pangs. Satiated I began my tasks for the day. It was 07:45.

Work was intense that morning, a deadline was approaching, and it required concentration and the minimisation of office distractions. Caffeine fuelled me as my hands and mind crafted solutions to the problems that presented themselves.

Without acknowledging the passage of time midday arrived, then bypassed me.

At 12:30 my concentration departed as I was presented with a dilemma: should I get some food or leave the office for a lunchtime swim. After briefly pondering the options I grabbed my rucksack and exited the building, moving in the direction of the swimming pool.

Exercise was important to me, I am not a naturally gifted athlete, built for power not speed, but through hard work and determination I had mastered a number of sports. Two marathons had been completed, a tattered belt of black was slung around my waist in my weekly karate sessions, three times a week I would plough through 500m with a combination of breast, front-crawl and butterfly strokes. I felt in good shape, my physiology outstanding.

Sliding behind the Royal Exchange I passed the Bank of England and descended the steps to the basement of a building which contained my gym and swimming pool. At reception I joked with one of the receptionists then entered the changing room where I removed my attire, placing my suit carefully in a wooden locker. I slid into my black trunks, placed my goggles on my arm and extracted my padlock from my rucksack, using it to secure the locker with a resounding click.

The key to the lock sat on a small carabiner, I threaded the waist cord of the trunks through it and secured both with a loop and a bow. From a pile of freshly laundered white towels I selected one and descended some steps and entered a corridor leading towards the pool. Mid way in my journey I entered a small tiled enclave and let the deliciously warm water of a shower cleanse my body. Shower completed I skipped up three long steps and walked alongside the pool to the end, nodding to the lifeguard.

The pool was calm, two lanes were occupied, and, unusually for lunchtime, the fast lane was empty. My breaststroke swimming style is strong not elegant and could not be described as quick, however, this lane was free, I would use it. I dropped from the end of the pool into the warm water, affixed my goggles and began my

500m. The swimming was tough, some days I glide, some days I struggle, that day in it was the latter.

500m approached and I switched to my least favourite stroke of front-crawl. Finishing with a flurry I rested at the end of the pool then pulled myself out. The air above the pool area was hot, it was a sweltering day outside. I moved to a recliner at the side of the pool, I wished to calm my breathing, to cool down, to relax before taking a shower and the return to work in my suit

I lay on the recliner for some minutes relaxing, my eyes were half closed and my pulse and breathing slowed towards normal.

And then it happens.

Nothing outwardly dramatic, nothing painful, nothing noticeable to others. I open my eyes and tilt my head to look at my chest, it feels as if something has broken inside, like a rubber-band snapping. A ripple of panic overcomes me, I know I am in trouble, that mortal danger is close, that desperate measures are required.

I am dying.

In one last act, one last final push, the last thing I do, the last thing I am capable of doing, I pull myself up from the recliner, hands clasped to my chest and attempt a scream.

The world fades. Reality disappears. I fall backwards across two recliners, my body motionless

My heart has stopped beating.
I am unconscious.
I am close to death.
Panic ensued.

People ran to me, help was summoned. Gym staff appeared, one takes charge.

I was lifted to the floor and rolled into the recovery position, a sensible move.

Yet I was not breathing. My heart was not beating.

The gym staff member in charge sensing this then rolled me onto my back, pushed his hands together over my breastbone and began compressions, squeezing my chest, forcing my blood to circulate, keeping me alive.

One round of CPR completed he rolled me back to the recovery position, I appeared to be breathing. I wasn't. This was agonal breathing, a brain-stem reflex. A precursor to death.

I began to turn blue. The cyanosis of oxygen starvation.

I was rolled onto my back and CPR commenced for a second time, my chest bending in response to the compression, my ribs cracking under the pressure. I was being kept alive.

A defibrillator appeared. Its rectangular white pads were unpacked and attached to me; one on my upper right chest, the other to my lower left rib-cage. A button was pressed and the automated device took over.

People moved clear.

A shock is delivered.

My body jolts.

My attendants hold their breath.

Watching.

Hoping.

Willing the shock to work.

My chest moves.

My heart beats.

I am alive.

I would not have survived the events of the 7th July 2016 without the intervention and tenacity of a number of people to whom I am eternally grateful.

The first on the scene was a member of the gym staff and he took charge of the situation, performing CPR and using a defibrillator on me – I would not be alive without him or his swift actions. I owe him a debt I can never repay.

The other members of the gym played their part in saving me, I cannot underestimate their contribution nor thank them adequately.

The paramedics who attended, their outstanding care, their expert diagnosis and transportation of me to the best heart-centre in London meant I suffered few after effects. I cannot thank them enough.

The doctors, nurses, hospital staff, cleaners, cooks, receptionists. I owe them so much.

The London Ambulance call handler who took the 999 call, who saw through the panic, who realised something was seriously wrong. Thank you is too trivial a phrase.

There are other people who played their part that day, people I was not aware of, am not aware of now.

To all of you I owe a debt of gratitude.

To all of you I owe my life.

David Jeffrey
Survivor
May 2017

ABSEILERS!

T he day had arrived, Saturday 24th June 2017, where myself and 8 other mad people including another 5 cardiac arrest survivors, met at The Arcelor Mittal Orbit in London's Olympic park at Stratford.

We were going to abseil down this lovely structure to help raise funds for various charities including SADS UK and the British Heart Foundation. In our group were of intrepid abseilers was myself, Ben Parkin, Gareth Cole, Michelle Edmonds and the one to blame for this , the lovely Trudy Bass-Chapman, all of us were the survivors. The others were Trudy's husband Ian, Brenda, Jo and Penny. Unfortunately, we were not allowed to take anything up with us that could be dangerous if it fell out of our pockets, so no cameras or phones.

Time had arrived for us to get ready for the abseil and then the journey to the top. We were ushered to a kit ready area where we were given equipment to put on; this included a harness which was rather uncomfortable when fully tightened (especially for us male participants). We had gloves to put on and also the important hard hat or safety helmet. The instructors advised on what was going to happen next.

We then made our way to the lift which would take us up to the top of the structure and to our final destination. We all seemed quite relaxed, no one seemed to be panicking or was asking too many questions, and in fact we were having a laugh. Finally, we arrived at the top and were lead out to our instructors who were up at the top. I and Ben had said we would go first but as it happened ben went with Michelle. So, I could stand back and see what was going on and how they were being made safe. Then time came for them to take the leap of faith (sort of). Ben and Michelle were ready to go for it. As we watched them go over the edge there were no screams or shouts just sheer joy that they were on their way down. It seemed like forever before it was my turn to take the plunge.

So myself and Penny climbed up onto the platform, did not want to look down, so just talked to the young lady that was going to look after me (she was braver than me). Eventually I was ready to go. So, with my back to the world and just looking at the Olympic stadium, I made the move to the edge. Gradually sat back into the harness and let the momentum take me over the edge.

Slowly, slowly, I heard the girl say, which I did; I was not going to do a Usain Bolt, no way, two foot, then one foot, then FREE as a bird. That moment was so wonderful and enjoyable, I just hung there and thought "this is wonderful" started to lower myself down, not to fast, steady away, all the while talking to Penny who was on the other rope.

We seemed to enjoy every minute of this. My emotions had gone, I was enjoying this too much. We were just taking in the wonderful scenery around us, seeing landmarks from a different perspective, canary wharf, the London Eye, the Thames and of course, the Olympic Park or for all football fans, West Ham United FC. Anyway we were nearing the bottom when I thought "I'll get brave", so I started to wave at my fellow survivors and relatives on the ground, and just hung there for a split second, then carried on down to the ground, I did just hang there, about 6 inches of the ground and was very proud of myself.

Finally, with feet firmly on the ground, I looked up to see what I had just accomplished and thought to myself, I am very proud to have completed this, and I would do it again, so for any other survivors out there that have not done something like this, I would say, "go ahead and do it, put it on your bucket list or to do list, you won't regret it".

So may I say a big HEARTY well done to the following: Trudy Bass-Chapman, Gareth Cole, Ben Parkin, Michelle Edmonds, Penny, Jo, Brenda and finally me, Chris Solomons, for showing that even if you have survived a cardiac arrest and some of us have ICDs, you can do anything you want to, within reason of course!

So BRING IT ON FOR NEXT YEAR.

Chris Solomons
Survivor
July 2017

A FRIDGE TOO FAR

Sunday 8ᵗʰ September 2013

There was nothing unusual that happened beforehand. No warnings. I hadn't done anything out of the ordinary prior to the event. In fact, I had had a pretty quiet weekend. I had stayed home Friday night. Saturday, I had done a bit of cleaning and food shopping and stayed home alone Saturday night. Sunday morning, I woke as normal and felt fine. I had one thing to do; a friend of mine had ordered a fridge from Argos in Meadowhall shopping centre and I had agreed to go and collect it.

I showered and set off for Meadowhall. On arrival at Meadowhall, I found a car park space very close to Argos and I remember thinking it was my lucky day. I had had nothing to eat so I decided to go to the food court for food.

Then I woke up, or rather I was woken up. I was in a strange room which I couldn't see very well. There was a man's' voice talking to me. I remember the voice but I remember very little of what was being said. I was being told not to panic. There was a woman there too. The voice said something about it being Tuesday. Nothing made sense and I knew it wasn't Tuesday, it was Sunday. I tried to remember where I had been last night. How had I got this drunk? I tried to move and then I felt people around me trying to stop me. They didn't need to because that's when I felt the pain. What the hell had happened to my chest and why couldn't I move without being in so much pain? Why did my head hurt?

As the weeks went on, I started to remember a bit more. I remember walking past Argos. I remember going into the food hall. I remember ordering roast chicken dinner and a large Yorkshire pudding. The food court had recently been refurbished by the company I work for. I remember looking around as I hadn't seen it before and I remember going to sit down and I remember where I sat. That's it. At no point do I remember feeling unwell at all. Everything from this point onwards until waking up in the hospital two days later, I have been told by the people involved.

78

I had been sitting on a high stool and I just dropped to the floor. I banged my head quite badly and someone near me thought I had been knocked unconscious by the bang to the head, but luckily for me there was a nurse sat nearby who had seen I was out cold before I hit the floor and had realised straight away. I had suffered a Sudden Cardiac Arrest (SCA). I had got some food lodged in my throat and even though I had fallen into a coma, I was choking. There was some confusion as to whether or not I was choking before I had the SCA. Again, luckily for me, the food court is next to the management offices and a well-rehearsed plan of action was implemented. The security staff got to me very quickly, the area was cleared, and I was brought back from the dead in five and a half minutes with a shock from an AED, and a team of 7 security guards, 2 police officers and the nurse who had been sat nearby.

Another team of security guards were quickly dispatched to every entrance by road to the shopping centre so that the ambulance could be directed to the correct place as quickly as possible. Also, because of the seriousness of the event and the location, multiple ambulances were dispatched in case the first one was held up. In the ambulance, I had to be shocked again as I suffered a further arrest. I have since met the paramedic who shocked me and he was delighted to see me as apparently, I am the third person he had shocked but the first to survive.

At this point I feel I should explain a little about my personal circumstances at the time. I come from a very small family, and I have no brothers, sisters or cousins. My mum passed away in 1989 and my only living relatives at the time were my dad who was then 84, and an uncle aged 78.

I had been separated from my wife for 3 years and she had moved to Malaysia. I was living alone, and working for a joinery and metalwork manufacturer where I had been for 18 years. I also owned a Thai massage shop which was originally my wife's when we split up.

The police and security at Meadowhall were in shock. They had brought me back, but I didn't look good. I had turned blue and my eyes had rolled, and they didn't expect me to pull through. A police car was sent to my dad and as he lived quite a distance from the hospital, he was sped across the city. He was taken straight to the Intensive Care Unit (ICU) where I had been placed. Before he was allowed to see me, he was taken into a room by a doctor and told that they believed that I had 50% chance of surviving; and that there was a good chance that if I did survive then I would have suffered some form of brain damage, and he should prepare himself that

I could be a very different person if I woke up. By this time, they had put me in an induced coma so that I didn't wake up too soon.

I had a few visitors while I was in a coma and later the nurse told me who had been but as with a few other things, I have forgotten who they were. One though, I will never forget. Thailand is a Buddhist country and Thai people are very loyal to their religion, and through the shop I have made many friends in the Thai communities so after I had woken up, it came as no surprise to me that a mystery woman had turned up at the hospital and stayed late in the night, holding my hand and praying. I had got a good idea who it was and I was right. It was a woman who I had been good friends with for a good few years but what made this particularly special was that she suffered with a fear of hospitals to the point that when she needed treatment herself, she wouldn't go to the hospital. To know that she has overcome this fear and sat with me was very special.

The days I spent in ICU are, to say the least, a bit of a blur and I can remember very little. The first visitor I had after I woke up was my friend and neighbour, Margaret. The police, not knowing I lived alone had gone to my flat as well as my dad's on the day of the cardiac arrest and as they were knocking on my door, she explained who she was, and they told her what had happened. From that moment on, Margaret was a star. She did everything that needed to be done; she let the shop know, she went and got my things back that I had on me although my clothes had to be thrown away as they had been cut to get to me quickly and I had been sick all over them (and one of the security guards as I learned later!)

Until this point, I didn't even know you could be sick while unconscious, but it seems you can so hey! I've learnt something. She let my workplace know where I was. I'd just put my flat on the market and she even contacted the estate agents and dealt with viewings for me. I hadn't been out of the coma very long when Margaret had come and apparently my first words were "How's the shop?" The shop was fine because Margaret had made sure of that too. Phones weren't allowed in there, but they made an exception so that Margaret could bring my phone to me and show me all the messages of support on my Facebook wall. I counted them later; there were 148. Facebook was later to play various parts in my recovery but for now I was still very dazed and weak, but it was nice to read them all and I managed to type a little post of my own. It simply said "I'm awake now. Thank you". I think I must have slept quite a lot for the following couple of days. I remember a guy I knew, but not well coming to see me and I found out he had blagged his way in by saying he was close family. I also remember that the nurse from Meadowhall came to see me, but I don't know who he was, and I fell asleep while he was there, and sadly, I have never seen him since. Hopefully, one day I might get to meet him to thank him properly.

After a couple of days, I was taken off the machines I was hooked up to and put in another room, but still with constant observation. I remember little about this other than I was in a lot of discomfort and none of it was actually my heart. I now know I had 4 broken ribs from the initial CPR, I still had my head wound, I had contracted pneumonia whilst in a coma and I had suffered 2 allergic reactions to medicines I was given when I was first admitted which had caused my neck and throat to swell up. I had developed a cough which isn't ideal with 4 broken ribs and I think I was probably asleep quite a lot of the time.

By now, word had spread around. I already explained I have very little family, but this makes me appreciate my friends more and I have always considered myself lucky to have such a large and varied circle of good friends. Although I didn't know it yet, many of them would play a part in my recovery. The nurses told me they were amazed by how many calls they had taken asking how I was while I was in ICU and by how many different people had come to see me. This could, however, have become a problem until Margaret stepped in again. She used Facebook to keep people updated so as to reduce the hospital calls and she organised the visiting so that I didn't have too many people there at once or periods with no visitors. This was no easy task as I have many friends from different stages of my past who don't know each other and not all of them were on Facebook.

By Saturday I was starting to come around more. My head wound had healed, my neck and throat were fine and my cough was a lot better, although I was coughing a little still and my ribs were still very painful. I still had no understanding of what had happened or how serious it had been. After all, in my mind nothing had happened. I'd slept through all the bad bits. One minute I was fine, the next I was waking up with what felt like the hangover from hell and the feeling I might also have taken a bit of a beating. I was starting to feel better, I was also becoming grumpy and irritable. This was partly due to my apprehension about being in a hospital due to a previous stay there 3 years ago. In 2010, I had a double hip replacement and my pelvis was reshaped. An operation which involved grinding part of the bone from my hip onto a powder to make a type of cement which was used to reshape my pelvis. During the operation, my sciatic nerve was damaged which resulted in a lot of pain, particularly in my right leg and foot, and the aftercare I received on the ward afterwards was, to put it bluntly, horrendous. I was on a ward used for people who had knee replacements and were only in for a day or so before they went home. I had no movement in my legs for 10 days and I was in a lot of pain.

The ward clearly wasn't used to dealing with someone in this condition. This was compounded by the fact that the ward was quite obviously very short -staffed, the staff they did have were run off their feet and stressed out, and the ward sister in charge of the whole ward had no people skills whatsoever. She reminded me of Hattie Jacques, Matron in the Carry On films rather than an employee in a modern hospital, and I was now dreading my stay in hospital after my 3 weeks of hell.

My fears turned out to be unfounded. This was to be another 3 week stay but it was the complete opposite experience. The care I received was exemplary without exception, and all the nurse's and ward sisters, the girls who brought food and drinks, were all lovely and I can't praise them highly enough for all the care I received this time round.

The main cause of my grumpiness though wasn't the fact that I was in hospital; it wasn't even the fact I had dropped dead a few days earlier, or the pain I was in from my broken ribs. I wanted my phone. I had been parted from my phone and I was not happy. Margaret had got it but I didn't know when she would be coming again. After everything I had been through, all I wanted was my phone. Nothing else in world mattered right now. Fortunately, help was at hand. My boss at work came to see me. He asked if I needed anything "Yes Nigel, I need my phone," I replied. "That's okay, I'll get it for you. Is it in the cupboard?" he asked as he moved towards the cupboard, "No" I said, "It's in a flat on the other side of the city". I have a very understanding boss and he agreed to drive right through the city in Saturday afternoon traffic to get my phone for me.

Once he returned I was a happy man. I was feeling better, I had my phone back and then, as I was improving I was moved onto a ward where I spent the next 2 weeks.

Switching on my phone was when I first got a realisation of just how serious this had been. There were 116 messages plus a whole new set of posts on Facebook on top of the 148 that I had quickly brushed through last time and bizarrely there were several WhatsApp messages from my separated wife in Malaysia wishing me a full recovery. It turned out that the hospital had her down as my next of kin from my previous stay, the police found her number in my phone. It was actually her old Thai number from before we were married, which she was using in Malaysia. Later, when I got my mobile bill, I found it cost me £34 for the call, but hey that will teach me not to keep my details up to date.

Reading the messages and Facebook posts in particular was a very uplifting experience, particularly the ones from when I was still in a coma. Realising how much people cared about you, seeing how much love they are showing you. In many of the posts, I could see and feel the shock and anguish that people were going through while I was lying there, having what, by now, I had started referring to as a little nap. People often say they would love to be at their own funeral, so they could hear what is being said about them. Well believe me, waking up from a coma after suffering an SCA and reading everyone's Facebook post on your own wall is probably about as close as you can ever get to that and it brought more than one or two tears to my eyes, let me tell you.

Now this may seem a strange thing I say, but I actually enjoyed my 2 weeks on the ward. The support and love I had received from friends was overwhelming and had really cheered me up. The staff were lovely, the food was nice. Margaret had brought me my own clothes from home and some of my friends were taking it in turns to wash them. Much to the bemusement of the staff, I had a constant stream of different visitors, both English and Thai. I had 3 friends who worked at the hospital and they came to see me regularly. I had books to read, and I was slowly replying to all my messages and chatting to people on Facebook. My boss had told me not to worry about work and confirmed that I would get paid for at least 6 weeks. The girls from the shop had been and told me not to worry about the shop, everything was fine. The landlord and his wife came to see me and told me not to worry about the rent. I was in a health scheme called Westfield, which would pay me £55 per day for each day I was in hospital up to 21 days. I had the rib pain and I got tired very quickly but other than that, I was fine.

I felt quite safe where I was. I was on the heart monitor so if anything else did happen, the nurses would sort it. The doctors did all sorts of tests to try and find a cause for my SCA, but found nothing at all wrong. At the time, this actually made me quite happy, because I had been checked over and everything was fine. I felt a bit like when I took my car for an MOT and it passed without needing any work doing to it.

The doctors were interested to know if anything had happened in the hours, days, months, and prior to the SCA which may give them some clues. They were aware of the report from Meadowhall that I may have been choking on my food, but no one seems to know for definite whether this happened or not. I had been under quite a bit of stress for the few years prior, but they didn't seem to think it was stress related, so in the end it was recorded as cause unknown [Idiopathic].

I was showing signs of minor brain damage. My speech was a bit slower, I could feel myself that I was not as quick as I used to be. My brain seemed to think more slowly and my reactions were not the same. I could tell the signs myself as I had been left with minor brain damage as a child, after a swimming accident in which I nearly drowned, and I was in a coma for a short while then too.

I was also forgetting things. One of my friends, when he came to visit me was aware my car was still parked in Meadowhall car park and he offered to go and collect it and take it home for me. Next time he came to see me, I asked him if he got my car home okay to which he replied, "Well, yes eventually, but it would have been helpful if you had given me the correct make, model, colour and registration number". It turned out I'd given him the number of my current car, but got 2 digits wrong and I had told him the make, model, and colour of my previous car from 3 years ago.

My heart had been quite stable while I was in hospital so my medication had not needed to be altered; so, once the decision was made to record it as "cause unknown" there were only two things left to do before I could go home. Fit an S-ICD and put me on a treadmill test. I became quite anxious as I was being taken to theatre and even more so, while I was waiting outside. It was quite a busy area and people seemed to be getting wheeled in and out all over the place. By the time I was actually taken into the theatre room I had managed to convince myself I was going to have another cardiac arrest and die. I hadn't been told much about the procedure and I hadn't asked, which was probably a good thing, as I found out afterwards it involved stopping my heart and letting the S-ICD do its job. Heaven knows what I would have felt like had I known this beforehand. As I was taken into the operating room, I was surprised at how many people there were there. At least 6 or 7, but the fact there was so many helped me feel a bit more reassured.

Later that day when I had come round, a nurse came to see me to talk to me about what was available afterwards. She gave me a number that I could call anytime for advice, a booklet containing details of local support groups but these turned out to be geared up more for heart attacks than cardiac arrests; and the meetings were during working hours so I never bothered with them. The next morning, I was taken for a treadmill test which was fine and that was it. I was free to go home.

I was told I should take things easy and rest as much as possible for the next 1-2 months and I was signed off work for another month and that I should see how I felt after that. It was office based rather than manual work which made a return to work easier. I asked if there was anything else I need to be aware of or avoid, and was told that once I had fully recovered, I should be able to pretty much lead the same life I had done before. I had to avoid contact sports, but I had to anyway due to the hip replacement. The only real change I had to make was my mountain bike, I used to put it in the back of the car and take it out onto the country bike trails; and although this was still possible, I was advised not to go alone and to always have someone ride close by; I was also advised not to ride on the road anymore; I was also told I would not be able to drive for 6 months from the date of the S-ICD being fitted, and I should contact DVLA as soon as possible.

My friend Liam came to pick me up from the hospital. It was a strange feeling I had. A bit like the feeling at the end of a holiday when part of you doesn't want to leave, and part of you is looking forward to getting back home. We didn't go straight home, I wanted to call in at the shop first which we did. This is where I found out how weak I still was. I stayed there less than half an hour and then Liam took me home. I was absolutely shattered by the time I got home. I'd felt fine in the hospital, but Hey! I'd been lying in bed all day or sitting in a chair and the most tiring thing I had been doing was walking to the toilet and back. Liam stayed a while and we sat talking, but I really needed to sleep so he left me to go to bed for a bit. Margaret had cleaned my flat for me so it was really nice to come back to, so I texted her to thank her and let her know I was home, but that I was going to sleep for a bit.

When I woke up, it had gone dark and that's when it really hit me. The hospital hadn't been real. I woke up remembering nothing about what had happened. I had left my flat 3 weeks previously to fetch a fridge. (My friend did get her fridge in the end in case you were wondering) and nothing in those 3 weeks had felt real. But now I was looking into reality. I was back in my flat on my own with sore ribs and wounds where the S-ICD had been fitted. I got up, put the light on, looked around and I cried, I kept on crying. I cried for over an hour. Then I went back to sleep.

I was up early the next morning. There was something very important I had to do. A friend was picking me up at 10am. We got held up in traffic due to road closures which was frustrating as I didn't want to be out too long as I knew I would get tired before long but this had to be done. Eventually, we got to Meadowhall; the first place we went was to the food court. I got shivers when I went to the spot where I had been sat, and even to this day, I still feel a little uncomfortable if I go to the food hall.

To me, Meadowhall will always be the place I was brought back from the dead.

Next, we went to find a security guard. We chose well as the guy I went up to introduce myself to, was Head of Security. He said 3 of the guys who had worked on me were working that day so he phoned them and asked them to come to the area where we were standing but he didn't tell them why. They all came but not one of them recognised me. I can understand why. The last time they had seen me was 3 weeks ago, to the day, and I was laid on the floor with my clothes torn off, in a coma, having turned blue and being lifted onto a stretcher.

My memory may not be quite what it was but the look on their faces when I told them who I was is something I will never forget. Nobody had told them I had survived, and the way I was when they put me in the ambulance, they hadn't expected me to. It was quite an emotional meeting. Under these circumstances, the words "thank you" just seemed so inadequate and I really didn't know what to say as I casually asked "Right, which one of you 3 broke my ribs?", two of them laughed and the other one looked at me sheepishly and said, "Sorry about that". I said, "Don't worry, I'm glad you did". Joking aside though, there were really no words to express how grateful I am to have seen these guys.

I later arranged a more official visit to go out and thank as many of them as I could. One of them was a professional boxer and I later went to see him fight. He won the fight but sadly broke his hand during the fight and hasn't fought since. We chatted for about 20 minutes or so and then they had to get back to work after posing for a few photos (for Facebook of course).

The next few weeks were a roller coaster of emotions. I tried to stay positive about things but it wasn't always easy. I was limited to what I could do as I was getting tired very easily. I had to accept that I needed to leave the shop to look after itself for a while. I stayed home most days; Margaret popped in regularly for a chat and to make sure I was okay, and some of the neighbours would pop round. My friends would come round and someone would usually take me to the supermarket if I needed it.

I started thinking about why it had happened. I didn't want to accept there was no reason for my SCA. I remembered a few things I hadn't remembered in the hospital. I remembered that on a couple of occasions over the past year or so I had felt a bit dizzy; once when I was walking down the street and I felt like was going to pass out, to the point where I fell into a shop window, but I didn't actually pass out. They were quite rare. I had remembered the palpitations and fast heartbeat I used to get occasionally, again quite rare. Previously, I had put these things down to being just something everyone gets from time to time but now I started wondering if they were all connected to my cardiac arrest. I started thinking about how likely I was to have another one and if I did, would the S-ICD do its job or not? Some days I could be quite happy and not worry about anything, others I would make myself more depressed purely by thinking too much. In the end, I convinced myself that the most likely possibility was the choking theory. I guess deep down I wanted to believe, this because to my way of thinking, if it had been brought on by choking, then it meant it was less likely to happen again and that was easier to live with, so I convinced myself this was the reason.

I sorted out some more practical things too. I contacted the DVLA and was told to send my license back. I sold the car and cancelled the insurance. They were quite helpful and told me my no claims bonus would be held for a period of 2 years and also, when I was able to drive again, having a previous SCA doesn't affect the cost. Sadly, the AA weren't so helpful, I still had 7 months of my membership to go and as it was going to be at least 6 months, I asked if I could either get the 7 months refunded or if they were willing to put my membership on hold until I got my license back, but the answer was a very strict no, and considering I had been with the AA all my driving life, I was very disappointed with them.

I got a call from the doctors asking me to make an appointment to see someone about my medication. I needed to anyway before my sick note ran out so I made the appointment. On arrival in the doctor's room, she made a mistake I have come to get used to. She referred to my cardiac arrest as a heart attack. Now I have to admit that before I had my SCA, I didn't really fully understand the difference between a cardiac arrest and a heart attack, so I can't really expect anyone else to, but I have been surprised that more than one doctor at my surgery has now referred to it as a heart attack and I am also very surprised at the lack of knowledge in general the GPs have about cardiac arrest. Not just GPs either. One thing that does annoy me a little is the way cardiac arrests are often reported in the media. I've known the top papers and the BBC, ITV, and Sky to refer to cardiac arrest as a heart attack at some point or another. She asked if I felt I was ready to return to work. I got the feeling that the decision was entirely down to me. In truth, I did want to go back to work. There are only so many episodes of Bargain Hunt that a man can take. In reality, though I was still getting tired quite easily and I think it would have been too much for me, especially as now I have to catch 2 buses, so I signed off for another 2 weeks.

Around this time, I received a text "Hi Baby, how are ya doing. I'm working in Sheffield this week" I'm not going to say much about this person as she is a very private person so, I will only talk about things relevant to the topic I am about to discuss, but basically she was someone I had met a few years earlier. We got on well and liked each other but she lived quite a way away from Sheffield so we didn't see much of each other. She had her life and I had mine, but she still came to Sheffield now and then; and when she did, she would sometimes stay with me on the Sunday before heading back home. This suddenly gave me another subject to worry about. Sex. It was something I had worried about when I first came out of hospital. Was it safe? Would it bring on another SCA? What if I overdid things? And the one I worried about the most, would an orgasm cause me to go into cardiac arrest? Then one night I came to the conclusion that if there was anything to worry about then surely the doctors at the hospital would have told me, so I decided to take the bull by the horn so to speak, and find out for myself. To my relief everything was fine. It still didn't stop me worrying though. She knew all about my SCA, I had contacted her whilst I was in the hospital and we talked a few times on the phone. Sunday came and she arrived at my flat mid-afternoon. We never went anywhere when she came, she would just come to my flat, I would cook something and we would just relax, eat and watch a film.

This time we didn't bother with the film. We talked a lot; this was the first time I had seen her since and she was obviously quite concerned and was asking a lot of questions, and I was telling her about everything that had happened. It was quite a while before either of us brought up the subject of sex and in the end, it was her who made the first move by asking "will you be okay for later?" I said yes, but I could tell she wasn't convinced. Anyway, the time came for bed and we took ourselves off to the bedroom. We started kissing but something just didn't feel right. I was a little nervous but I think she was a little scared too.

I should also say at this point, there were a few instances prior to my SCA where I had lost my erection, and she had already suggested I went to the doctors and ask for some Viagra, but I hadn't got round to doing it. Tonight though, it was obviously not going to happen at all, so we just lay in each other's arms talking. The next morning, I made another appointment at the doctors. It can be potluck at my doctors, which doctors you can see but fortunately on this occasion, it was a man. He couldn't prescribe anything there as he didn't know if it was safe for me or not. He would need to contact my heart specialist at the hospital. I did get them prescribed before her next visit though. Again, I went through various thoughts in my head so I decided it was best to take one first on my own so I would feel better about them when my friend was there. They seemed to work fine so I was quite happy when she visited again. The tablet did the job, but something still didn't feel right. It was quite a while before I saw her again. I didn't know it, but this would be the last time I saw her. We still texted each other for a while but she never came up again and then we gradually lost touch.

It's been over 3 years now since I last saw her. I came to realise what went wrong later, all the fears I had about sex were all perfectly natural after what I had been through, but somehow I had confronted them and overcome them, but I had done it on my own. She had exactly the same fears as me and she was scared for me, and what might happen to me. I'll never know if I had been more open and talked about this, whether it would have made a difference or not but I had learnt a very valuable lesson, that if I was I was to have any sort of intimate relationship with anyone in the future, I would need to be more understanding of how they were feeling and learn to be able to talk about these feelings with them.

I decided that I was ready to return to work after the current 2 weeks had ended. By this time, it would be 9 weeks since my SCA. My ribs had just about healed, I still got tired a lot but I was certainly a lot better than I had been. Bargain Hunt hadn't got any better. I'd tried changing channels but Jeremy Kyle just wasn't an option. So, another doctor's appointment was made. They weren't able to let me go back to work until they had discussed it with my heart specialist, which they did and they agreed I could go back to work, but I had to start on reduced hours and gradually increase them each week, which my employers were happy to do. So, it was agreed I would work like this until the end of the year and then back to full time in January. I was also given a less stressful role on a temporary basis to help me get back into the swing of things. I did find it extremely tiring at first, especially as I still had 2 buses to catch each way. One thing I noticed straight away, when I went back to work, the company had got photos of many of the jobs we had done on site and described to make the best ones into larger photos that could be hung on walls in the office. Now when you walked into the main office, there is not only a huge photo of the Food Hall in Meadowhall, but it's the actual area I was sat in when I had my SCA.

In 2014, things started getting back to normal. I still had minor memory problems and I would still get tired a lot more easily than before. I sometimes get panic attacks, sometimes palpitations and I could sometimes get dizzy. Often when any of these things happened, I would suddenly start to feel weak and tired for a while afterwards. On one occasion, while I was walking through the local market, I started to feel dizzy and light headed, and my heart was beating quite fast and I went to customer services and asked if they could let me sit down for a bit. They said I didn't look good and called an ambulance for me. The paramedics did an ECG and my heart was okay but still beating fast so they took me into hospital as a precaution. The staff in A&E were really good. They monitored me for a few hours and my heart had returned to normal. They were very understanding and told me if anything like this happened again, I should always go to A&E to get it checked out if

I was worried. I was to do this once more in the year and again, the staff were really good and everything was fine. Generally though, life was good. I had settled back in at work, I changed the way the shop was run, so it was entirely run by the staff and didn't need me there much. I sold my flat. The plan was to move into the flat above the shop at the end of the year, so I went to live in a friend's house for a few months which was a lovely place on the edge of Sheffield, backing onto the countryside. I still went out drinking and socialising, although I was careful not to drink too much, unlike my life prior to the SCA, and I was living a virtually normal life. If anything, I had become a bit too complacent and wasn't taking care of myself as well as I should have been doing. I was also forgetting to take my medication on various occasions and not worrying too much about it. I'd got my driving license back and I had bought myself a new car.

On New Year's Eve 2014, I moved into the flat above the shop. Then I went out to celebrate the New Year. I stayed out quite late into the morning but I was careful not to overdo it with the alcohol. I woke up about 11am on New Year's Day. I was feeling quite tired and lethargic but I'd had a very long day the day before, so I decided today was going to be a rest day and I stayed in bed watching TV and reading. The next day I still wasn't feeling up to much. I got up and unpacked a few things and did a bit of cleaning but generally I had another lazy day. My friend who lived across the road from my new home texted me and asked if I wanted to go out for a drink that evening and I said yes. We had a few drinks in the pub and then we went over to a place across the road that is basically a place with pool tables, table football and TVs above a shop that stays open until 6am. I was feeling a bit tired and wasn't even feeling like having a drink and in the end I left my drink and went home. When I got home, I realised that I hadn't had anything to eat for 2 days. No wonder I wasn't feeling so good, so I made myself a large bacon sandwich before going to bed. Probably not a good idea as it gave me indigestion. Something else I hadn't done, although I hadn't realised it yet was I hadn't taken any tablets in the last 2 days.

I woke up with a start about 8am and 3 things were all happening. I had the most horrendous indigestion (It definitely was indigestion and I knew it was as I suffer with it quite frequently due to the medication). My heart was racing very fast. In fact, it felt like it was a lot faster than it usually is when it goes fast. I was very tired and I wanted to go back to sleep but I couldn't because of the other things happening. I tried to go back to sleep but it was hopeless. My new room has an en suite, I got up to go the bathroom and BANG! Like lightning. Literally. I can't be 100% sure but I think I even saw a blue spark in my chest because the room was in darkness. If you can imagine taking a very severe blow to chest, but the pain and the force from the blow were on the inside, and it lasted just a split second. The force had knocked me into the wall. My S–ICD had fired! Sheer panic set in. I screamed. I found the light switch and looked for my phone. My heart was racing more than ever now. I went into the kitchen. BANG! This time there was no wall so I fell onto a chair. There was no one else in the flat. This was it. I was going to die. I was still screaming. I found the keys to the back door. The door opened onto a metal staircase which led onto a small backyard. There was a door at the back which was the entrance to a house and at the other side was a bakery which was part of the Chinese cake shop next to my shop. I stood at the top of the steps shouting. I got the attention of the Chinese bakers who came out.

To this day, I don't know if they have recovered from the shock of watching me standing at the top of the stairs in just my underpants, screaming and jumping about at them and making jerking movements when I was shocked for a third time. They certainly didn't understand I was trying to get them to call an ambulance because I was about to die. I went back inside and I got a fourth shock. I found my phone and dialled 999. I had my fifth shock which turned out to be the final one, just as the guy who lived in the house at the back came running in after hearing my scream. I was told by the 999 operator to sit down and try to stay as calm as possible until the ambulance arrived. It was there in minutes. I felt a bit better as soon as they arrived and my heartbeat was going slowly back down again. I was taken into hospital where I was diagnosed as having gone into Atrial Fibrillation (AF). It's not life threatening but my S–ICD didn't know that and more to the point at the time, neither did I. I am not going to talk about my experiences with AF here as this story is about my SCA and I don't believe it's relevant here. Maybe one for another story- and I had pretty much recovered from my SCA when it happened. It did however lead to an increase in the number of occasions I got palpitations, fast heart beats, and panic attacks and I also started getting ectopic heart beats which, combined with my previous SCA, I found very difficult to deal with emotionally, at times. Over time, I learnt to cope with these better. I learnt to take care of myself. I take my tablets at the correct times every day without fail. I make sure I get enough sleep, I make sure I eat properly and I try to eat plenty of healthy food although I do eat plenty of rubbish as well at times, and I always make sure I drink plenty of fluids although I now avoid alcohol completely and try to limit caffeine by only drinking decaf coffee. This has gone a long way to helping me live a normal life that I now lead.

My final subject is Facebook groups and one group in particular Sudden Cardiac Arrest UK who are the reason I am writing my story. Not long after my SCA, I was talking to a friend about the lack of help and support there seemed to be for people in the aftermath of an SCA and she suggested looking for a Facebook group. I did a search and found 2 or 3 which I joined. I didn't find these to be much help however, and in fact, on occasions, I think they actually made things worse. For a start, they were predominately American and the American Health system is completely different to that in the UK. They also tended to be about heart conditions in general rather than just SCAs, which meant I was reading posts that weren't really relevant to mine. Combined with the American way of dramatizing everything some of the posts were actually scaring me rather than helping me. I was then invited to join a group called British Hearties. I was a lot more comfortable with this. It was British so hopefully I would get to know people closer to home who had suffered an SCA in similar circumstances to me. In some ways, this was a good group, the guy who ran it was nice, there were loads of people on it but it was a very general group; it covered all aspects of heart health and there seemed to be very few people who had suffered an SCA. There were a few helpful posts, but it was more for people with heart related issues to get together and talk about anything and wasn't really what I was looking for.

Then I came across a group called Sudden Cardiac Arrest UK, this group ticked all the boxes. It was started by a man named Paul Swindell, who had suffered an SCA himself. It was a fairly small group which suited me and which was to be expected as the chances of actually surviving an SCA are very slim, especially if you are not near a defibrillator; and it is made up entirely of people who have survived an SCA. There is professional support available on the group, the people in the group were friendly and all the posts are related in some way or another to the subject of SCA or the SCA Group. I found the group to be very informative and helpful. It was also a very positive group. I found all the other groups to be quite negative, but the people here were different; they were all dealing with their SCA in a positive way and rebuilding their lives despite having had an SCA, rather than letting it control their lives, and I took a lot of strength from that.

An added bonus was that they held occasional meetups. This, I was particularly excited about as I had never met anyone else who had survived an SCA before. The next one was on a Saturday in London. The distance wasn't a problem to me as I had a friend I could stay with down there, so I decided to make a mini break out of it and spend a few days in London. The meeting was to be held in a room above a pub in Southbank. There was a small charge of £5 to cover part of the cost of the room and the buffet which was provided. The rest was paid for by SAD's UK charity which is a charity set up to help prevent sudden cardiac death. The day of the meeting came and I was both excited and nervous, I was looking forward to meeting other people who had gone through the same as me. I was also a bit nervous. I knew some of the group knew each other already and I had come alone. However, one of the group members was staying close to where I was staying so I arranged to meet up with him the day before and that helped me on the day. At least I would know one person when I got there.

However, I didn't need to have worried, everyone in the room was really nice and friendly and easy to talk to. It felt as if our SCAs had formed a bond between us even before we had met. As you have already read, I have had all the help I needed from my family and friends, and I really don't know how I would have coped without them, but at the same time I was the only one who knew what I was going through and I had to deal with a lot of it on my own. Suddenly, for the first time I wasn't alone; I was in a room full of people who had been through it as well. I found it very beneficial talking, listening to people's stories and telling my story.

It was easier than talking to my friends and others around me. There were many things that didn't need saying, didn't need explaining, because we were all talking to people who can understand them already. Everything was so positive too. These were not people who were going to let their SCA ruin their life. They had faced or were facing the many issues that the aftermath of an SCA brings, and were determined to live life to the full. I left feeling very inspired and positive, and with a bit more confidence about the future than I had before. Since the meeting, the number of panic attacks I get has reduced considerably and I am quite certain, this is due to how I felt meeting and talking to other survivors.

There is very little support available in the UK post SCA and SCA UK is providing something that is desperately needed. I have been more than happy to sit down and write my story for them. I hope that people who have had an SCA will find it helpful; that they can read it and realise some of the things they are going through are just natural and that they are not alone. Once you have had an SCA, then it never really goes away, even if you are lucky enough to make a complete recovery physically, there will always be some mental and emotional issues and it's a continuous learning process dealing with them. I have tried to be as open and honest as possible, not just about my SCA, but about the issues I faced afterwards, no matter how well or badly I dealt with them. I hope that others will read it too and understand a little bit more about SCAs and also think about what they can do to help. I am one of the lucky ones. I was near a defibrillator and people trained in CPR. I have a story I can tell. Most people who have an SCA only get a funeral.

Have you a business that has an external wall where an AED can be mounted?

Would you be willing to raise funds to have one fitted or even fund one yourself?

Learn CPR so that if someone close by you or even family and friends suffer an SCA you could perform it until help arrived. CPR won't restart a heart that has stopped due to cardiac arrest but it will keep blood and oxygen flowing and help avoid serious brain damage.

I also hope that some of my friends will get to read this at some point and if you do, please know I appreciate everything you have done and continue to do for me.

I love you all.

Bob Reville
Survivor
September 2017

THE SUN WAS SHINING ON THE LAST DAY OF LIFE

O f course, that morning when I woke had no idea that at ten past one that afternoon I would be dead. But it is like this for everyone else, we don't ever awaken thinking that this will be our last day. We may joke about it, profess to do things, make statements about changing our lives as "I could be dead tomorrow", but as we say these things, make these pronouncements, we don't actually believe that this will be the case. It's just a figure of speech, it will never really happen.

But, of course, for me, for us, it did.

For we are the victims of sudden cardiac arrest, where for some reason (and, for some, no reason) our hearts stop pumping, our world turned to black, the fog of clinical-death engulfed us in its arms, the nothingness of death embraced us.

And yet, we are the lucky ones.

We are the ones that lived, the ones for which an almost infinite random sequence of events, the what-ifs, the if-onlys, meant that we returned to the living, left death's lingering caress behind.

And, lucky as we are, for many there hangs a mist around us, an emotional discourse left unsaid. For some, the victory of returning to life, the joy of resuscitation is tainted by an unquantifiable sadness, an emotional upheaval that defies expression.

Our lives are inexplicable altered by our event. The old person, the old "I", literally dies and is replaced by a new one. Yet we are still the same person, but we are different, the contradiction apparent.

But we must enjoy our new sunrise, our new breaths, our animation. And although our lives are different we must embrace the joy of now, of being here, of being loved, of feeling pain. For we know the alternative, we have observed the void, travelled the abyss.

We must truly embrace life, for we know what it is like to experience our last day.

We must cherish the sunlight.

David Jeffrey
Survivor
August 2017

ENJOY LIFE

My wife and I have just returned from a holiday, the first since my SCA 1 year 11 months ago. We booked a 3-week fly drive in North America, passing through numerous National Parks to celebrate us both reaching a "significant 0" age.

Before going, I can't deny that I had numerous concerns. Would I still be here, would I be legally allowed to drive, would I get travel insurance, would the holiday be "too much" for my body, would the airport security checks be a problem, would the long flight be OK and finally would being at altitude during the time in the USA cause me problems? A lot of my concerns were answered just before we went, the ICD technicians and my GP, both said for me to get out and enjoy it. My GP gave me extra medication because the prescription was due to run out during the holiday.

My insurance company was a bit more of a problem, two weeks before departure and after the ICD had undergone its 6-monthly check, they then sprung it on me by email, that they were happy to provide cover as long as the person responsible for my treatment said they were happy. (I chose to check with them that I did have cover for the USA with my declared condition because I simply do not trust insurance companies and I wanted something from them in writing in addition to their terms etc.) As I have not seen the consultant since my discharge from hospital, then who was responsible? To cover all angles, I managed to get an OK from the consultant who treated me in hospital in time, (only because a friend of mine works alongside him). I told him exactly where we were going and what I wanted to do and the altitude.

The airport was no problem, the 10-hour flight was no issue at all. My experience of being at a mainly 6000' above sea level in the USA for just short of 3 weeks turned out to be no more a problem for me than being at sea level. I actually went up as high as 10,500 feet. I checked trails and their severity before we left the UK and made a route before we left.

All of this took time and planning, but it turned out to be worth it. I accept that there were some places I did not consider trying to get to see, I knew the trail would be too severe. While going to those places I did go to, I just took my time and listened to my body whilst carrying 10kg of my camera equipment.

So, what is the point of this post?

Don't let the SCA stop you doing things, it's a beautiful world we live in and you can still get out and see it if you choose to.

Enjoy life.

Mick Schofield
Survivor
October 2017

FOUR ICD'S AND A DODGY VALVE

I woke up in a hospital bed in the CCU ward of the Royal Free Hospital on 22nd December, 1994. My wife, Adele, was sitting beside my bed and I asked her what was happening and where was I?

I had arrived at my office the previous morning to collect some files, and had just stepped outside the door onto the pavement when I collapsed, unconscious, on the pavement. My employer saw me lying there and told one of the staff to dial 999. I wasn't moving or breathing and was just lying there on my back, going grey. While waiting for the ambulance to arrive, he knew he couldn't just watch me die and, having seen CPR being administered once before, he decided to have a go at it with me.

A paramedic on a motorcycle arrived in about 8 minutes and, luckily for me, he had an AED with him. He began prepping me for a defibrillation procedure when a 2nd London Ambulance arrived with two more paramedics. It took them about 30 minutes to get something resembling a stable output from my heart. On the ride to the hospital, I arrested 3 more times, receiving defibrillation each time.

Once in the resuscitation unit, I was stabilised and my wife and daughter arrived to see me lying there, covered in foil insulation and with all conceivable wiring and machines hooked up to me. My daughter told me later that the 1st paramedic was waiting outside Resus in a very nervous state as he had only qualified 6 months earlier and I was his first SCA to survive. I was sedated and kept unconscious for a further 24 hours.

Once I awoke the next day, the cardiology team confirmed I had arrested but couldn't say exactly why. They did tell us that I could not be discharged until an ICD was implanted. My wife arranged a transfer to St. Bartholomew's in London where I was cared for by a specialist arrhythmia team. I had recovered all my senses except for short term memory and was feeling quite strong and well for another month and my ICD was implanted in late January 1995. I left the hospital within a week and continued my recovery at home.

Not a lot of information about life with a defibrillator was available in those days. We just got on with things. I lost my driving licence and was unable to find work until the following April.

In the meantime, I almost arrested once in my sleep and then, in March, I arrested at home in front of my 8-year-old son. The ICD paced me and I regained consciousness but was still in fibrillation. Then, the ICD went off with a full defib shock and restored my heartbeat.

The ICD went off twice more that year but I wasn't in ventricular fibrillation. The doctors fine-tuned the ICD and prescribed a beta blocker for me and everything went back to as near normal as possible under the circumstances. I endured another cardiac arrest whilst asleep at home in January 1999 and was saved by my ICD giving off another lifesaving shock.

No further arrests have happened since and I am now on my 4th ICD. The eventual diagnosis of my arrests suggested that my prolapse mitral valve, which I was born with was at fault and I received an artificial mitral valve via open heart surgery in December 2003. I continue to live a fairly normal life, taking only two drugs for life; Sotalol Hcl (beta blocker) and Warfarin because of having a carbon fibre mitral valve in my heart.

I have an excellent prognosis so far. My initial arrest occurred at age 46 and I will be 70 next February. I am currently an outpatient at Harefield and have a Boston Scientific ICD (my 4th) and a bedside monitor now. It does an automatic upload and transmission to Harefield every three months and I have an annual appointment there for the pacing clinic, my cardiologist and an echocardiogram, as well. I have no serious issues regarding this exciting medical story. I got my driving license back just over 2 years after the initial arrest and have been flying all over the USA and Europe ever since. I've lived to see two of my children get married and there are now 3 grandchildren that I might never have seen.

A few technical points to add...

My 1st ICD was implanted in January 1995.It was a Medtronic unit and weighed over one pound. It was inserted into my abdomen below the left side of my ribcage. The sensing/pacing leads ran up under the skin over my rib cage, up to my collarbone and then entered an artery to go down into my heart. It took me about 6 weeks to begin sleeping properly because of the bulge over my intestines. I did get used to it, and, although I couldn't ignore it altogether, it did get more comfortable. That unit went off 4 times, twice saving me from SCAs and twice inappropriately, knocking me off my feet whilst fully conscious. It was replaced due to battery getting weak in March 1999.

The second one was about the same size/weight as the first and was also inserted into my abdomen in the original pocket. Everybody still with me? I don't remember the manufacturer anymore. That one never had to go off and its battery began to go downhill in 2008, just before my daughter's wedding in August. This surgery was done at Harefield and while discussing the procedure with my cardiologist, he realised he had forgotten where mine was. When I reminded him it was my abdomen, he laughed and said things had moved on since 1999. The new one would be implanted in a pocket behind my left pectoral muscle; it was that much smaller! That was done in late July 2008. I don't remember the make of that one, either.

Finally. ICD #4 was done in September 2015 and one of my leads was failing, so a new lead went in, as well. This unit is a Boston Scientific, accompanied by a new bedside monitor. It's about the size of that cigarette lighter (a Zippo I've had since my Air Force days).

So, that's 23 years' worth of ICD technological progress. This new one is invisible behind the chest muscle. I'm the only one who knows exactly where it is. The only negative side of all this is that they left # 2 in my abdomen because they weren't going to subject me to 2 procedures back in 2008. So, they just switched it off and it sits happily and quietly in my guts. Again, I'm only aware of it because I know exactly where it is! Apart from the relatively unnoticeable scars from all the incisions, I don't look like I've had all this surgery done on me.

To finish, finally, my dodgy mitral valve began giving up on me in 2003, and I underwent open heart surgery in December of that year and received a carbon fibre mitral valve to replace my failing one. That's now only evident by the fading vertical scar over my sternum (breastbone).

Mark Wendruff
Survivor
October 2017

TAKE THE FIRST STEP

I am writing this for all the right reasons in the hope it is well received and through it some people might sense the art of the possible. I am not writing it for any egotistic reasons or to solicit any endorsements for I have far too much humility for that.

I previously wrote a post called "Dare to Dream" in November 2015 when the group was much smaller than it is today. Although I am not sure if it's still available I suppose this is a follow on post from that?

I had my SCA in June 2013 at 4am in the morning while fast asleep.

A sleep I never woke from but my then partner Dawn for some reason of fate stirred, woke up and realised I had suffered from some form of catastrophic cardiac event.
She did all the right things by calling 999 and commencing CPR and eventually my heartbeat was restored with a defibrillator operated by a skilled paramedic.

I know I am extraordinarily fortunate as indeed we all are who survive an SCA.

A week in a coma in ITU followed by a two month stint in hospital where my hypoxic brain injury affected most of my functionality for example my co-ordination was that of a toddler thus walking, holding a spoon to feed myself, washing or even wiping my arse was all beyond me.

Listening to someone speak and then understanding what they said was all but impossible and my memory was shocking. In fact I could retain data for at least as long as a Goldfish before having to ask people to repeat information again and again and again. I thus did abysmally on the psychological testing that all brain damaged people go through in order to know how badly they have been affected. I just could not find my way through the maze or put the brown bear into the cage. I was thus diagnosed with hypoxic brain injury resulting in poor executive skills, poor attention span and poor memory.

I was bed ridden so I peed through a catheter and did a No 2 into a bedpan after which some unfortunate had to wipe my bum. Bet they loved that Job!

In fact I was a mess riddled with myoclonus (involuntary jerking) that was so bad one day I jerked so ferociously I landed on the floor next to the bed. For those who do not know Myoclonus is similar to when you are on the verge of sleep and suddenly for no apparent reason you jump. Only I did that all the time while awake or sleeping, and the muscle pain is considerable, akin to severe cramp. Give me a spoon to eat with and moments later it would be a missile because I had jerked. The ice cream I was supposed to eat decorated all the walls around me because I could not control my arm movements to feed myself.

The realisation that I was seriously damaged and it wasn't everyone else being idiots smashed my confidence to smithereens and at that point if I could... I would have killed myself.

I looked at the ward windows with both fear and longing but I couldn't get there because I couldn't walk or crawl, so I planned my suicide and planned it again and again because 2 minutes after I had made a fantastic plan I promptly forgot it and had to plan it again, but of course then I would forget what it was I was supposed to be planning?

It was indeed a very low time for me.

Two months later they sent me home with an ICD and a wheel chair and made arrangements for community physiotherapy and psychological re-evaluation. Six months later I received an appointment with a physiotherapist and shortly afterward a letter from the psychological evaluation team telling me my appointment had been cancelled. I immediately wrote back an angry letter cancelling any future assessment not realising that by doing so my hospital notes would forever state that I had hypoxic brain injury and needed an appropriate adult to accompany me on all future appointments.

Sometimes I am such an idiot!

Six months after coming home I also received a shock from my ICD at about 4 in the morning. Subsequent investigations revealing that I suffer from mild sleep apnoea which may trigger cardiac irregularity. Just another thing really?

When I look back on this period in my life I realise that Dr's are skilled and wonderful human beings but they are not gods, and they don't know everything. Unfortunately, they are expected to know everything so when they are asked a question that they do not know the answer to, they guess...

Dr, How long am I going to live?
Dr, Will my wife still love me when I get home?
Dr, What are next Saturdays lucky lotto numbers?

They will try and answer by giving a calculated guess based on what they think they know and what it is you are hoping to hear. Well I asked questions that I have since forgotten together with the answers but what I do remember is how as a result my personal confidence was shattered, spat on and ground into a pulp. I thought I am alive but yet my life was over because now I am the village idiot (ever had that feeling? I hope not) I left hospital brain washed with half-baked opinions that I took as gospel because Doctors know everything and everything they say is true! Reminds me of the theory of voodoo when I think about it!

By way of example I was told that you improve for two years and after that you have got what you have got. Simply not true you continue to improve forever long you live and the more you try to improve the more you will improve. I was told that my mobility would not improve to the point of independence and I would need a person or carer to accompany me when I ventured out.

Wrong!

My mobility has improved and I do not need an adult or carer to accompany me when I venture out. When in ITU my relatives were told I would probably die and when I didn't they were told I would probably be a cabbage?

Not something grand like Asparagus or a Truffle but a bloody cabbage?

I now realise that if you sustained hypoxic brain injury as I did/have then with time other parts of the brain take over that missing functionality. As in my case you may have to re-learn how to do things but you can re-learn and be as efficient as you once were.

You really can!

To be fair to the Doctors my balance was blooming awful and once I became ambulant I fell over frequently, but as time has passed my balance has improved, so although I still fall over I fall over much less than I did which is fantastic! Then again I am 61 years old and thus four years older and of course balance degrades with age but my cunning plan is to take up yoga (more of that later)?

So why am I writing this?

Well after I had gone home from hospital and sat wasting my life away watching daytime television for long enough I got a little angry. I realised that I had bought into the despair of having an SCA. That I was no longer capable, that I was forgetful and clumsy I got angry with the Doctors and nurses who implied how limited my life would be. But most of all I got angry with myself for buying into these beliefs and for feeling permanently depressed, for wasting what years I had left watching Cash in the Attic and Bargain Hunt and for well... frankly believing that my life was over and I was just... waiting to die.

The truth is that this isn't true and it's a mistake to believe this rubbish!

Life isn't over, indeed far from it!

After my anger had subsided I came up with a cunning plan and we sold or gave away pretty well everything we owned which was both a bitter sweet experience. It was hard parting with things we had owned for almost all of our adult life. Useless things that were mementos of some person, event or experience.

Note that all these things refer to the past

But we did it, cried over the loss and then next day celebrated the freedom because everything you own sort of owns you back in a way doesn't it?

Now at this point I should say that I am writing this post on a table top in the saloon of a yacht that we bought in October 2015 and sailed with my wife, (yes my wife Dawn who last year I married on a beach in Australia) from New Caledonia to Australia then Indonesia and now we are currently on route across the Singapore Straits to Malaysia and then Thailand

Having been told I had such a poor future I manage to undertake all the maintenance, service the engines, replace and tune electronics, plumbing, calculate routes and pretty well everything else that it helps to know when running a boat.

When I embarked on this journey I honestly didn't know if I could do this or not because I still believed all the hype and my confidence was shattered. Indeed, I didn't know if I could fly halfway around the world to even look at a boat I was interested in that was for sale. It was in a boat yard and I didn't know if I would be able to climb the ladder to get onto it let alone sail it anywhere?

But as doddery as I think I was I managed it and we bought it.

Since buying it we have sailed it to some wonderful places and seen some wonderful things that if I remained at home I would never have undertaken or seen.

If I had of failed it would have been sad but then I would have taken up golf, fell walking, camping, gone to college to learn something new or whatever. I would have done something that gave me a belief that I had a value because it's important to feel that we have a human value whether it's in building a house, looking after the children or grandchildren or growing lovely tomatoes in the garden.

As a side I take Bisoprolol to regulate my heart and my Medtronic ICD sits happily in my chest. I have a home monitoring kit which I plug in and charge up as and when I need to do a six-monthly download, I can walk, run a short way with wobbling difficulty and remember my name and a few other things. I don't dive but I do snorkel on the many reefs that we have anchored near and I have seen some wondrous things.

My stamina has improved because it had to, my balance has improved because it had to and my joie de vivre (love of life) is now as it should be.

I am writing this because I sincerely believe that far too many of us experience an SCA and believe the hype that we cannot or should not do anything which might endanger us. That life is somehow restricted and now dominated by hospital appointments, physical and most of all mental limitations that we impose on ourselves.

Utter crap!

What is the point of living if we let our SCA confine us to an ill state?

We worry about falling over in public or having an ICD shock in the cinema or feeling unwell at a party when these are all our own fears no-one else's ?
The truth is if you fall over most people are concerned and want to help.

When I told my Cardiologist I was buying a yacht and going off sailing he truly belly laughed. I often think of that when I go swimming off the back of the boat in amongst the Turtles and Clown fish or watch a perfect sunrise.

But when I asked him if I could do a tandem skydive in no uncertain terms he vigorously and expressly forbade it, so I suppose there are limits?

An SCA can ruin your life, it can destroy your confidence in yourself, it can take away your livelihood and test your relationships, and it can leave you feeling depressed, suicidal, unloved, sexually inadequate, useless, helpless and hopeless. We all know it can do lots of negative things?

But you also can do lots of positive things because you are not dead you are still here and you... yes you... have all the tools you need.

You are alive, you have skills unique to you, you can think and you can do, and it's a fact that most things in life that we consider impossible is because we haven't yet tried them?

Oh yes the yoga?

During my travels I have met many wonderful people one of which is a middle-aged woman who taught yoga. Well in all honesty I felt a bit of a plonker lying on a mat bending this or twisting that amongst a group of ladies but I watched this teacher almost balancing on one toe while standing on the end of a pencil and my jaw dropped in awe! I was sold on the obvious benefits so I thought as we are hoping to sail to Thailand where yoga is huge, and hopefully spend a while there, I am hoping to go to yoga classes to learn how to control my balance better.

At least that is my ambition?

I hope I haven't made this all sound very easy because it certainly has been anything but that! I have fallen off the boat some 10ft onto concrete and got away with grazing and some bruising. Fallen off the boat during the night in heavy seas and got tangled in illegal fishing nets. Got smashed to bits at the top of the mast when I had to go up there to sort out an emergency and came down looking black and blue and I have reached levels of exhaustion that have really tested my metal. I have clearly forgotten things and had to relearn after mistakes were made but fortunately nothing terminal.

The rewards have been immense, but at times it's been a hard thing for me to do but I do feel that my balance has considerably improved, my stamina increased and my confidence enhanced.

If you are like I was when I watched daytime television lost in the abyss of depression thinking your life is over then please think again because it isn't. But you have to take that first step and as a clever Chinese guy once said, "Every journey of a thousand miles begins with the first step".

Whether it's growing potatoes or spending a dawn watching the sunrise from the gardens of the Taj Mahal it's up to you to take the first step?

Richard Houghton
Survivor
October 2017

STUBBORN OLD GIT ONE YEAR LATER

W ell the last time I left a note was a couple of months after my SCA in September 2016. By November I had also suffered a pulmonary embolism caused in part, the doctors thought, by the implanting of my ICD. So, after another stay in the emergency unit I was put onto a blood thinner, Rivaroxaban and sent home when all seemed well.

A week later I was feeling good and got up in the morning and went for the obligatory emptying of the bladder and lo and behold I nearly had another SCA when I pee'd blood instead of the usual, so much that I thought I would faint. Called the wife who called NHS who booked us an appointment for the next day in the hospital.

We had to get a cab to the hospital and went to ambulatory care ward, one look at the sample we had taken with us and was told "you are not going home!!" So, another ten days being prodded poked and cameras inserted where men really don't want them inserted (my bladder was very clean on the inside), I even won a bet with the senior urologist when I insisted that there was nothing wrong with my waterworks and why didn't he talk to my cardiologist about the blood thinners. So, after him paying his debt to me (which I donated to the ward) I caused no end of fuss being a stubborn old man and insisted I be transferred back to cardiology.

Back on cardiology and all went well and dosage of blood thinner reduced and home I went. Was seen by the cardiac nurses who said, well you certainly know how to keep us on our toes and again I told them that I was not going to give in or up. A week later I found myself with breathing problems, initially I put it down to having maybe twisted a couple of the mending broken ribs. I looked at myself in the bathroom mirror and noticed I had white nipples!!! So, call the wife, who called the cardiac nurse who was there within the hour who listened to my chest and said - I think you have pneumonia!! So, another blue light trip, because by this time I really could not breathe without any oxygen mask. At A&E there was much joking about "Your usual bed sir?" and "Did you pre-book for this week's stay?" etc. Anyway, guess who had picked up a hospital acquired viral infection which then led to the pneumonia and pleurisy? Eventually, I was released from hospital on December 10th.

Four life threatening occurrences later and the cardiac team were calling me Mr Miracle, in their experience no-one had been able to survive so much post SCA and still be smiling. Well, to say I took it all in my stride would be boasting and a lie, but here I am one year later and now in 18 days, I, my wife and family (who by now all have a small amount of PTSD) pick up the keys for our adapted dormer bungalow near the sea. It's been a tough year, perhaps more so for my wife, son and daughter, but we have got through it. There have been some very down moments and some great laughs, we have wonderful friends who have supported us. The damage to my heart is severe, left ventricle only works at 15% so getting enough oxygen to my brain means sitting down most of the time. But I have my driving licence back and a whole new area to discover at our new location on Anglesey, I was lucky to only suffer minimal recent memory loss so although I might forget what I ate yesterday I still have all my pre SCA memories. You will get down and fed up and it can be very hard, but try for humour and being aware that there is another go at life. If you can be positive about what has happened.

It's a wonderful life for a stubborn old git!!

Keith Lord
Survivor
October 2017

FROM PALLBEARER TO PAIL BEARER

My working life has been quite varied with no direction of a career choice (hotel trade, estate agent, prison service) until about 4 years ago when I started working in an office in a shop part time. The premises also housed a funeral directors and part of my job as an admin assistant was to complete estimates, invoices, in memoriam donations and process payments for the funeral department.

Over time I became more involved in the funeral side of things to the point of preparing the deceased, liaising with families, clergy and printers etc. and also pallbearing at funerals. About 5 months before my SCA I had started to train to become a funeral director alongside my admin duties for the shop and funeral department.

It was a job where I felt I had found my vocation in life and I really enjoyed being part of a process that means so much to people and prided myself on doing my job well. All that changed after I suffered SCA on 6 October 2016. I wasn't fit enough to return to work for several weeks, but in-between Christmas and New Year I decided I was well enough to go back on a phased return.

I was kept away from the funeral department and some of my funeral duties but was just about managing my other duties. The fatigue was still pretty bad at that time and my memory wasn't great but still I carried on. Then, one day I was in the staff room (which looks over the funeral yard) and I saw one of the operatives wheeling an empty coffin from the workshop into the chapel of rest and had a vision of myself laying in that coffin and consequently I went to pieces. It was then that I realised that it was too soon to be back at work (I had managed almost four weeks) and I went home an emotional wreck. Over the next few months I cried a lot of tears thinking that my career was over, and I suppose I grieved for my "old" life. Around this time, I had some trauma counselling which helped a little.

Jump forward six months and I had come to terms with the fact that I may not be able to return to my old job as I can't cope with it emotionally. I was medically dismissed in April this year (2017) once my sick pay had ceased. It was then that my experience with the benefits system took a turn. I was able to claim some additional benefits (I'm a single parent so get some on top of my wages) and I was told I could claim employment and support allowance (ESA) to cover the wages I had lost, which I did. I also had to attend health assessment 20 miles away from home (which was a problem itself due to some anxiety) where they would decide what I did or didn't qualify for to claim from the DWP.

As a result of that assessment I sit and write this blog, a little frustrated about the situation I have been backed into. The DWP told me I didn't qualify for ESA and that I should claim either income support or universal credit to top up my existing benefits from HMRC. After speaking to another department at the DWP I was informed that I didn't qualify for either of those and should make a claim for Jobseeker's Allowance and would be expected to be actively seeking work and attend weekly or fortnightly signing-on appointments. I was told I should also attend workshops for writing CVs and perfecting interview techniques, etc. on top of the signing -on sessions. All such appointments in town 15 miles away, sometimes attending twice weekly. I was told that if I didn't attend I wouldn't get any money! I was already struggling to pay my rent in full (thankfully having kept my rental agent informed they were very helpful) and put food on the table. It's quite scary not knowing when your next money will be coming in or how much it would be and worrying that I would be evicted if I couldn't pay my rent going forward. I could feel myself becoming anxious and stressed. While I was dealing with all the phone calls, appointments etc. I saw an advert on social media for a job as a cleaner within a brand new local domestic cleaning business, so I decided to message the owner and was invited to go in for a chat.

Living in a small town where everyone knows everyone, the lady I saw was already aware of my SCA story and as I explained what I needed she said she could accommodate my requirements! Wow, I couldn't believe it. I had bagged myself a job with the hours I wanted without even having an interview as such and I started a couple of weeks ago (4 days before my 1st SCA anniversary). The first few days have been tough going and I was really nervous about whether I could cope physically with the strain due to the lingering fatigue and muscle wastage of the ICD implant in such a busy and physically demanding job. I needn't have worried as I coped reasonably well. I made sure I had early nights and kept my fluid levels up and ate when I needed to (I feel very strange when I get hungry, not like I did before the SCA).

Ultimately, I'm looking forward to getting back out into the world. One year (almost to the day) post SCA and I feel like I'm getting my life back. Despite thinking I wasn't ready physically or emotionally to go back to work, I think I actually am, and I've surprised myself with that. I have been told repeatedly by various people in the medical professions that it can take at least a year to recover from a trauma such as an SCA and, by golly, I've realised they are right.

As I enter the second year of my recovery I look forward to the challenges that my new life will throw at me. I'm feeling happy and positive for the first time in what feels like forever! I know it's not always going to be straightforward but with each little milestone I am gaining confidence and strength and will get fitter as time goes on. I am now also working with a team of similar aged people that I have things in common with. Making new friends and acquaintances adds to the positive direction my life is taking at the moment. Go me!!

I can only encourage other survivors to step out of their comfort zone and take the plunge into new or unknown areas as it definitely boosts recovery.

Ingrid Gardner
Survivor
November 2017

ONE DAY IN JULY

The sun was shining on the last day of life. Of course, that morning when I woke had no idea that at ten past one that afternoon I would be dead. But it is like this for everyone, we don't ever awaken thinking that this will be our last day. We may joke about it, profess to do things, make statements about changing our lives as "I could be dead tomorrow", but as we say these things, make these pronouncements, we don't actually believe that this will be the case. It's just a figure speech. It will never really happen.

However. For me. It did.

July 7th 2016 began like any other day. The alarm clock on my bedside table announced itself to the world at 05:35, its shrill tones interrupted my slumber. I rolled over and grabbed the device, sliding the front-panel switch to the off position, silencing its interruption. Sliding out of bed I staggered towards the shower, my eyes bleary, the July daylight seeping around the roof blinds, bright shards of light illuminating my journey.

The hot water of the shower soothed my body, washing away the vestiges of my slumber, under the jet I replayed the events of the previous evening. I had played in a band on stage for the first time ever, playing guitar and singing, my nervousness at the performance had been superseded by the elation of being the bands front-man and producing music that people enjoyed. The elation had stayed with me and as I exited the shower I was humming my band's tunes in my head.

Drying myself and partially dressing I descended the stairs to my home-office, located on the ground floor. The house, constructed in the 1940's was of a chalet style, the sloping roof meant limited storage options on the upper floor. My suits and shirts were, therefore, stored in a built-in cupboard in my office on the ground floor; unconventional but practical.

I selected my number-one suit, a dark-blue Ede and Ravenscroft two-piece and put on the trousers. I selected a white shirt, slipped in collar-bones and then blue cufflinks. I slid into the shirt, then pulled a blue patterned tie off a hanger and then tied it in a half-Windsor knot around my neck. I slipped on burgundy loafers, grabbed my suit jacket and headed out of the house. It was 06:55.

The drive to the station was uneventful, no other cars appeared at this early hour. The sky was clear and the sun, which had made itself known to the countryside some hours earlier, hung low in the sky, long shadows from trees added to the beauty of the early morning. I parked at the station, placed my car-park pass on the dashboard, slipped my jacket on and strode towards the platform, my band's tunes still in my head. At the station coffee shop I greeted the servers, their faces had provided a reliable backdrop to my daily commute for the last six years. Coffee in hand I moved to the platform and took my place in the queue.

The train journey to London took place in silence. Commuting at this early hour was the role of regulars, the rules of this being no talking during the journey, this time was ours and the peace was appreciated by all. I read the day's news on my phone and plugged in my headphones and listened to music. With the low sun and early hour the views through the carriage window were tranquil and inspiring, the English countryside at its best.

On arrival at Waterloo I exited the carriage and after a brief walk along the platform descended into network of walkways linking the platforms with the underground network. Progressing through the ticket barrier I then walked down a long ramp to the platform of the Waterloo and City line, and, after a short wait, got on the underground-train that stopped, empty, to let the commuters board. The Waterloo and City trains are small, noisy, grubby and hot, designed for the sole purpose of shuttling between Waterloo and Bank station in the City of London which they did adequately.

Arriving at the surface opposite the Bank of England I walked along a pedestrian only road toward me office. The City has a buzz to it, hard to describe unless you work there, that morning it was almost visible as people like me progressed towards their offices.

Swiping my security-pass through a barrier allowed access to my building and one lift journey later I arrived at my desk on the seventh floor of the building. I was time to start work. However, on this particular morning I was very hungry. My 05:35 start was too early for me to eat, my body is not receptive to nutrition at that early hour. And now, at 07:45, I felt the hunger pangs, my body required sustenance.

My building contains a restaurant in the basement so I descended in the lift and filled a plate with food, a paper cup with coffee and sat and ate a welcome meal. Replete I ascended once more to my desk. Now it really was time to begin work.

I am a physicist by training and spent part of my youth working for CERN in Switzerland, in the days before the LHC and Brian Cox had made the place famous. Much as I appreciated my academic career I was born in the wrong era for a permanent job and when my fixed-term contract ended I was forced to look at other careers for employment. I had an aptitude for IT, or computing as it was then referred to, so I returned to the UK and followed my nose from one role to another in this field. Although I now worked in the City I was a latecomer to the environment, at my age and experience I was at the top of my game in IT and the City provided the financial rewards commensurate with this.

I worked for an asset-management company which dealt with the investments and pensions of a large number of savers. My job was to produce software systems for the management and optimisation of these investments, so, replete after my breakfast I set to work.

The morning disappeared underneath a flurry of work and mid-day approached, then that too disappeared. At 12:30 I stopped work, I was hungry again, the desire to eat made itself known to me. My lunchtime routines varied, but on two to three days a week I would swim, an exercise I most enjoyed. In my mind I weighed up swimming versus eating and, whilst almost wavering, decided that I would swim. I picked up my blue rucksack which contained my swimming gear, put my wallet into its front pocket and headed to the lift.

My walk from the building was pleasant although the coolness of the early morning sub had turned into the ferocity of its mid-day incarnation. I moved quickly, eager to get out of the heat and below ground level, and I passed in front of the Bank of England before descending three flights of stairs into the basement containing my gym and swimming pool.

I am not a naturally gifted athlete, I am built for power rather than speed. But through training and determination I had mastered a number of sports. I wore a tattered belt of black in weekly karate sessions, I had recently run two marathons, I was fit and in good shape. Swimming was my favourite sport, however, and, in all my years of gym membership I had never once used the gym, I had the gym membership to get access to the swimming pool.

I joked with the receptionist at the gym before entering the changing room. I removed my suit and shirt and placed them carefully on hangers, put on my trunks and locked everything safely away in a wooden locker. The key to the locker I looped through the drawstring of my trunks which I tied in a bow. As of habit, I placed my goggles over my upper arm and walked towards the pool. Prior to the pool I dodged into a shower and washed myself briefly under the hot water, then, ready for my swim I walked up some steps and to the end of the pool. I nodded towards the lifeguard, he was familiar to me and vice-versa. Normally I would swim in the centre medium lane, however, today this was occupied. The fast lane was empty. I would not class myself as a fast swimmer, however, it was the only free lane so I dropped into the pool determined to justice to the lane's speed during my 500m swim.

I ploughed up and down the pool using my favourite stroke of breaststroke, however, for the last four lengths I switched to front crawl, making every effort to keep my body horizontal and to glide rather than splash through the water. As I finished the last length I was breathless, although this was nothing unusual, I had exerted myself and this was part and parcel of exercise. After pausing for a minute I heaved myself out of the water and walked around the end of the pool towards the pool exit. The air in the pool seemed warm, mirroring that outside, so I decided that I would rest on a poolside lounger and let my respiration and heart-rate return to normal before taking a shower and putting back on my suit. I wanted to avoid being out of breath and hot and sweaty in my work clothes.

I lay on the lounger as my breathing returned to normal, my heart rate was still high but was slowing.

And then here, in this tranquil scene, in the mundaneness of me lying on a plastic lounger next to a swimming pool, on this nothing-out-of-the-ordinary day in July my life ended.

As I lay on the lounger I was oblivious as to what was about to happen, I had no warning, no pre-existing signs or condition. But at around 13:10 a clot blocked the left circumflex artery of my heart causing a myocardial-infarction (heart attack) and this was enough to bring on ventricular fibrillation (cardiac arrest) where, instead of my heart's chambers beating in sequence and pumping blood around my body they quivered chaotically and pumped no blood at all.

I sat up quickly on the lounger, my hands clasped to my chest. It felt as if a rubber-band had broken inside. No great pain or discomfort just the realisation that something was seriously wrong, that my heart was not beating. I attempted to scream, but it was too late, I collapsed backwards, unconscious.

At 13:10 on July 7th 2016 I was clinically dead.

It was fortunate that I had sat up, in doing so I turned through 90 degrees and placed my feet on the floor, so when I collapsed I fell backwards across two loungers and not simply back on the lounger I was sitting on. Had I not done so it may have looked like I was asleep and the outcome would have been different. This was the first of the random pieces of luck that saved me that day.

It is not clear whether my shout was audible but my collapse had been observed and the lifeguard along with another swimmer ran over to me. At this point I was lying across one lounger, my back on the floor, my head propped up on a second lounger. The lifeguard radioed for help then attempted to assess what had happened to me.

I was displaying the outward signs of agonal respiration. This a brain-stem reflex triggered by low oxygen levels and indicates someone is close to death. The signs I displayed were myoclonus (my left arm was shaking uncontrollably) and I had what appeared to be laboured gurgled breathing. The lifeguard, having never seen agonal respiration before mistook this for me having a fit, the seriousness of what was happening was not apparent to him.

Alex the building-services manager appeared. He had observed the events unfold on the CCTV monitor in his office and came running. He was not meant to be at work that day, but had come in to attend to some matters. This was the second random piece of luck that day which saved me.

Alex took charge of operations. He, too, initially, thought I was having a fit, however, with the aid of other swimmers he lifted me off the lounger and onto the floor and placed me in the recovery position. He also, via his walky-talky, instructed for an ambulance to be called and he summoned the gym's defibrillator. The third piece of luck that day was the gym was equipped with a defibrillator and all the staff were trained in its usage.

My face turned blue and the myoclonus ceased and it became apparent that I was in a serious condition. Alex rolled me onto my back and observed my chest, looking for signs of breathing. He placed his head me my mouth as he attempted to pick up signs of exhalation. He was worried about starting CPR in case I didn't need it, that, indeed, this was simply a fit. However, after his observations he decided that this was the only course of action. He placed his hands together over my breastbone and back to push rhythmically. My chest creaked and bent in response to his actions, my heart forced to circulate blood.

After a minute Alex stopped CPR he thought that I had started breathing, although my body remained lifeless and limp on the swimming pool tiles. Checking my breath he rolled me into the recovery position, but this efforts had not been sufficient, I was completely motionless and a blue-grey pallor overcame me.

Alex pushed me back onto the floor and recommenced CPR. This time, from the strength of his arms and from the force he applied my sternum and ribs cracked. The sound, as it was described afterwards, was similar to a wooden chair breaking. On each push from Alex he forced blood from the chambers of my heart and into the arteries, the circulation produced by CPR is far poorer than by a beating heart but is enough to have some effect on the body. My chest cracked and creaked as Alex pushed, the rest of my body remained lifeless.

A tense looking member of the gym staff appeared with the defibrillator and he knelt by my head placing the unit on the tiles. He carefully unpacked the defibrillator pads whilst Alex continued with the chest compressions. One pad was stuck on my upper right chest, the other onto the left hand side of my chest. Alex and the others stood clear as the defibrillator analysed my current status.

The defibrillator, detecting that I was in VF announced that I was to be shocked and that people should stand clear. They moved away and held their breath.

The defibrillator delivered a shock. Its effect on my body was immediate and dramatic. My chest shook, my arms and legs lifted from the tiles, it was if I had been kicked into the air.

The question for Alex and the others was whether the shock had worked, whether it had reversed my demise.

My chest began to move, awkwardly at first and then rhythmically, my heart was beating and I was breathing.

At approximately 13:17 on the 7th July 2016 I achieved ROSC: Return of Spontaneous Circulation.

Alex had achieved the holy grail of resuscitation.

I was alive.

I started to move, then to writhe as consciousness returned, my arms moving randomly. Alex tried to calm me, aware of my confusion and he gently pushed my arms down. I was told to lie still, that help was coming, but this was confusing to me, being oblivious to the events of the previous seven minutes. My brain, trying to process what it perceived lead me to be convinced that I had simply fallen over whilst getting up from the lounger. A brief conversation to that effect took place with Alex, who, with a calm sereneness reassured me that everything was going to be ok and that I just needed to lie still. Comprehension of the situation that I found myself in seemed impossible. I sat up and immediately felt the effects of the chest compressions on my ribs and sternum, the pain palpable. Alex calmed me and got me to lay, once more, on the tiles.

Two paramedics dressed in their green uniforms, appeared, they carried resuscitation equipment in two shoulder bags. Alex explained what had occurred in the previous minutes and there was some incredulity on the part of the paramedics that I had been in VF arrest some minutes earlier. It was not normal for them to attend a cardiac arrest where the patient was either ROSC or fully conscious; I was both.

Two more paramedics appeared. The 999 call handler had seen through the panic of the call and had concluded that something was seriously wrong at the gym, a suspected cardiac-arrest which warranted the dispatch of two separate ambulance crews. In addition, an advanced paramedic, upon hearing the call decided that something didn't sound quite right, and decided to attend. This was the fourth piece of random luck which saved me that day.

The defibrillator was examined by the paramedics which allowed them to determine that I had been in VF arrest and they slipped into a well-rehearsed routine. For the majority of cases where the victim is unconscious the protocol is to heavily sedate the patient, to intubate them (place a plastic tube into their throat to aid breathing) and to transport them to hospital. My case was unusual in that I was conscious and able to communicate, therefore there was no merit in heavy sedation nor intubation. ECG electrodes were placed on my and the paramedics looked at the trace with interest. The heart rhythm, although not fully stable indicted my heart was beating normally. An in-situ ultrasound scan of my chest was performed, firstly my chest was shaved by a paramedic then the functioning of my heart was observed on the ultrasound monitor.

It was assessed that I was stable but in pain so a cannula was placed in my right arm and morphine and midazolam injected. Research had shown that cardiac-arrest victims with ROSC had a better chance of survival if left in-situ for fifteen to twenty minutes to let the circulation return to normal and the body's systems to normalise, so I was kept, lightly sedated, by the side of the pool.

Outside the gym, at street level, traffic chaos was in progress. The three ambulances had parked directly outside the gym blocking the road to buses and other traffic. A police-car was parked adjacent to the ambulances, not realising that the gym had a defibrillator the 999 emergency services had requested the attendance of the nearest vehicle with a defibrillator, London's police cars are equipped with devices so had attended.

After a period of stabilisation I was moved to onto a stretcher and the tortuous route out of the pool and back to the gyms reception was skilfully navigated. The gym contained a small lift, and, again, with skilful manipulation I was loaded into the lift and arrived back at street level. Exiting the building it was eerily quiet. The street runs towards the Bank of England and is a major thoroughfare for buses and taxis, and was normally filled with loud slow-moving traffic, and yet, here, on my way to the ambulance there was none. I queried this with a paramedic, he responded that the police had closed the road, that the ambulances had caused a blockage and that they had rerouted traffic. In fact, the traffic chaos caused by this extended three miles in all directions.

The chief paramedic attending to me, had, by this point, assessed my situation, had a fair idea of what had happened to me and decided that I should go immediately to Bart's Hospital into their specialist cardiac catheter laboratory rather than be taken to A&E. This, as it turned out later, was the correct thing to do, that my left-circumflex artery could be fixed and I would avoid issues that a delay going to A&E could have caused.

The blue-lights flashed and the sirens blared as the ambulance hurtled the short distance to Bart's. Upon arrival I was taken from the ambulance directly to the third floor of the hospital where the catheter-laboratory was. The chief paramedic had telephoned ahead and a team had been assembled ready to take me. I was wheeled into one of the theatres (labs) where this medical team took over. Blood was taken for assessment and I was found to be hypokalaemic (low blood potassium) although, post arrest, my physiology had gone haywire.

Consent for surgery was taken from me and I was prepared for the angiogram. This is procedure where a special dye is injected into your veins and, in real time, x-ray images are obtained of the heart, beating; the operation of its arteries and their health can be assessed and action taken if they are blocked.

I was disconnected from the paramedic's ECG machine and connected to the hospitals. A cannula was fitted to my right wrist as a hollow needle was inserted into the radial artery. This was done to allow a balloon and stent to be inserted should that prove necessary. I was then placed on the table, whilst a robotic x-ray camera swung over me and the diagnosis began.

Most of my arteries appeared in reasonable health with no major blockages, however, the scan by the medical team was systematic and precise and a narrowing of my left-circumflex artery was observed. A stent was prepared, and via the cannula in my right arm was inserted into the artery on the end of a line. The surgeon skilfully moved the stent along the artery in my arm and towards my heart, where, negotiating the branches and turns of the coronary arteries it as located at the narrowing of the left-circumflex. The balloon was inflated and the stent placed at the narrowing, opening the artery and letting the blood flow unimpeded.

The rest of my arteries were checked and it was deemed that no further action or stents were required. No further drama was necessary. From the catheter-lab I was wheeled to the cardiac High Dependency Unit (HDU) and placed in a bay close to the nurses for monitoring.

From my cardiac arrest, to resuscitation, to transportation by ambulance to Bart's, to being stented and to cardiac HDU had been approximately ninety minutes. On the 7th July 2016 I had survived cardiac arrest.

Aftermath...

My sojourn at Bart's was a week long. Initially I was stable and the only discomfort I felt was from my cracked sternum and ribs. Unfortunately, as I was an MI victim I was prescribed the standard protocol of medication for this which included Bisoprolol, a beta-blocker, at a dose of 10mg. This had the effect of relaxing my heart, however, it also had the effect of lowering my pulse rate such that it hovered around 30 beats per minute. After four days in hospital and with an erratic pulse hovering around this figure I was faced with the mental challenge of "this is how it ends". This was more my perception of the situation, not the medical staff's, however, I faced the oncoming doom one night, expecting the inevitable at any point. Come breakfast time the following morning I realised that I had been overly pessimistic.

On discharge from hospital I returned home and visited my GP. There was a look of incredulity on his face, it was impossible for him to comprehend that this healthy looking man sitting in front of him, had, one week previously, suffered cardiac arrest. This was not the fault of the GP, it is just a fact of life, there aren't that many cardiac arrest survivors, and, prior to publicly available defibrillators there were even fewer, so GPs very rarely saw a survivor.

Fortunately, being an MI victim I was assigned a cardiac-rehabilitation course which comprised a boot-camp style exercise class, aimed mainly as MI victims who had not exercised regularly before. With my level of fitness I was confident that the course would be easy. My arrogance preceded my capability. A combination of the after-effects of the arrest and the medication I was taken meant I found the course very tough to begin with, which I found difficult to accept as two weeks prior to this I had been capable of running seven miles with ease.

My sleep pattern was disturbed, I would awaken early and could not get to sleep again. I also found getting to sleep difficult. Something was buried in my subconscious in that as soon as I fell asleep I would wake up suddenly, convinced my heart had stopped. This would repeat itself twenty or thirty times. I also found when lying down that my heart rate fell and was more erratic so for many nights I would sleep in an arm-chair, sitting in the chair raised my pulse reducing my paranoia.

I continued the cardiac-rehabilitation exercises at home but found running difficult due to the beta-blocker dose but spent more time cycling.

Tiredness was a problem, caused, I believe, by the beta-blockers, but I didn't fight the tiredness, if I needed to sleep I would simply sleep.

After approximately seven weeks I went back to work. Three days a week to begin with and then to five after a few months.

My hypokalemia was investigated but no cause found, it must have simply been a result of my physiology going haywire during and after my arrest.

I did not appear to suffer hypoxic brain injury although I did go through a phase convinced that I had! I found my short-term memory affected and was sure this was due to a brain injury. However, it is likely this was an after effect of the midazolam given to me by the paramedics. I suffered the same memory issues when given this medication a second time for another procedure, so am of the opinion that I did, indeed, survive, without a brain injury.

I was not unaffected by the arrest. As anyone who has suffered cardiac arrest it is almost impossible to explain to someone who hasn't what it is like and what it feels like to survive.

One day in July changed my life forever.

David Jeffrey
Survivor
December 2017

YOU CAN

I had a "cold" in December 2015. Being a typical man, I disregarded my loving wife and continued my 90 hour week as always in that month including the absurdity of a family trip to Sydney and a high-pressure US trip for Raytheon. Points on the BA Gold card... so, I cooked Xmas dinner as always complete with trimmings etc. and that cough just would not go away.

December 27 I agreed to be "hassled" by my wife Kim and go and see the on-call GP. This was, as was proved to be lucky, at St Mary's in Paddington. I never saw the GP. Instead I had an SCA next to the lift. That was my last memory of 2015; "I think I need to sit down darling"

Little did I know I had raging pneumococcal pneumonia which had gained sepsis to help it to basically kill me. At the time my lungs were 90% damaged. 6 rounds of CPR ensued after my wife screamed and got a doctor out of the ladies room. I got to visit the special room normally reserved for the Royal Family and was in an induced coma for several weeks.

That was the easy bit!

I woke up and everything was a bit different... I too had that pesky Action Myoclonus thing, otherwise known as Lance Adams Syndrome. So, I essentially went from retired RAF Fighter Pilot, decorated senior officer of 20 years and senior engineering Manager to a 2-year-old baby. I hit myself in the head with my spoon when I could pick it up. Could not stand, forget walking.

So, there it was. Life over. I too dreamed about suicide innumerable times when in the Charing Cross Neural Rehabilitation Unit (CNRU). Every day was another failure to meet my own standards.

What next, I hear you ask?

Piracetam and lots of it, dampened the shaking and jerking. 8g, 3 times a day at that time. The maximum. Lots of physio and eventually release 24/3/16. With wheelchair. Special toilet seat, handrails and swivel bather. Daytime TV as per Richard and eventually Physio/ OT outpatient care.

Quite a lot of despair and utter rejection of love ensued. Amazing who you can hurt, just because they care... I discovered that Alcohol makes everything go away... life, love, and hope. No one needs them huh?

Clearly, that's not the end; just the start.

We now live in Sydney, I have loads of nephews and nieces to spoil. I catch every cold going because I have no immune system, Myoclonus never goes away. I get scared of crowds, transport and anything that changes my routine. I'm blessed because of what I have now. I might have changed; but that's all. My wheelchair is in my Mum-in-laws garage. I'm a house husband who bakes a mean apple pie if he can avoid stabbing himself! I have a 30-year RAF Reunion to go to next week in the UK and I shall.

Am I scared?

Damn straight!

Shall I do it?

Equally.

You CAN

That is the start of my new story.

Ian
Survivor
December 2017

MORE INFORMATION

You can find more information about Sudden Cardiac Arrest UK and its members on the following online platforms:

See our website for all sorts of useful information, branded merchandise and the blog where many of the included articles were first published:

SuddenCardiacArrestUK.org

Facebook is our primary tool for social interaction and we have several options.

For Survivors and those directly affected by an SCA come and join our GROUP for social interaction, chat, sharing of stories, etc. at:

Facebook.com/groups/SuddenCardiacArrestUK

If you haven't been directly affected but have an interest or would like to support us please "Like" our PAGE at:

Facebook.com/SuddenCardiacArrestUK

If you are a medical professional, have an interest in the Chain of Survival or have performed CPR or used an AED on another then try our sister group Chain of Survival UK:

Facebook.com/groups/ChainOfSurvivalUK

HELP US

We are currently run on a voluntary basis and any financial burden has been borne by private individuals and more recently by SADS UK. We'd like to grow and build our organisation so that we can do more and stand on our own two feet. Until we are able to do that any donations made to SCA UK will reside with SADS UK in a ring fenced account. Any funds donated for SCA UK purposes will be used in accordance with SADS UK and charitable organisation rules. If in future it is deemed that SCA UK is in no need of any funds raised they will be ceded to SADS UK.

If you would like to support us financially you can make a donation through our Just Giving page at:

JustGiving.com/fundraising/sca-uk

And by purchasing any of our branded merchandise:

SuddenCardiacArrestUK.org/shop

If you have found this book of value we'd kindly ask that you leave a five star review on Amazon and also maybe on our Facebook page.

If you feel suitably inspired and want to document your own sudden cardiac arrest story we'd love to take a look and hopefully we can share it on our blog or maybe even in a future volume of Life After Cardiac Arrest?

* * *

Printed in Great Britain
by Amazon